THE KIDS' COLLEGE ALMANAC

A First Look at College

Barbara C. Greenfeld

Robert A. Weinstein

GERSON

Matawan, New Jersey

Page xv: Excerpt, reprinted with permission, from *The Phantom Tollbooth*, by Norton Juster, © 1961, renewed 1989, A Bullseye Book published by Random House.

This book was set in Times New Roman, Hot Air, Weissach, and Helvetica.
The editors were Julie R. Kerr and Deb Cohen; the design consultant was Margy Kuntz;
the cover design was by Leslie Gleason/Phoenix Concepts, Inc., and Tom Dounelis;
the production manager was Coordinated Design.
BookCrafters, Inc. was the printer and binder.

Quantity discounts are available on bulk purchases of this book for fund raising, educational use, premiums, or gift giving. For details, please contact the marketing department at Gerson Publishing Company.

The Kids' College Almanac: A First Look at College.

Gerson Publishing Company
P.O. Box 525
Matawan, NJ 07747

Library of Congress Catalog Card Number: 95-82244
ISBN 1-888584-00-9

96 97 98 99 00 01   8 7 6 5 4 3 2 1

To Larry,
who has lovingly helped me through
life's many tollbooths,
even when I haven't had exact change,
and to David and the Chunkman,
who from the start
brought special love and meaning
to life's journeys and adventures.

B.C.G.

To my teachers,
Joan C. Keenan,
who gave me a love of learning
to last a lifetime,
and Mary Lee Ruddle,
who gave me Chaucer's Prologue,
Dylan Thomas' snow,
and a tow line for the blizzard.

R.A.W.

To Mom and Dad,
with love.

B.C.G. and R.A.W.

THE KIDS' COLLEGE ALMANAC

Contents in Brief

THE KIDS' COLLEGE ALMANAC

Contents

14   WHAT SHOULD I DO NOW?   231

Preface

Kids think and dream about the future—or at least other worlds different from the ones they occupy at any particular moment. They experiment with all sorts of roles. Young kids run around with capes, hats, and other dress-up clothes, imagining themselves to be everything from Frankie the Fireman to one superhero or another. Imagination and experimentation then move to the more traditional—doctors, teachers, moms, dads, and other roles borrowed from the adult world. Anything and everything seems possible.

When you're in fourth grade, it seems quite reasonable to be a professional athlete who then becomes a doctor and finds the cure to a terrible disease, or a model who is also a movie star and an astronaut. Through middle school, kids continue to talk about challenging, meaningful, and even daring careers.

Kids are the ultimate optimists, often even in the face of extreme adversity. Some literally embrace the motto "The sky's the limit!" They achieve goals that bear a striking resemblance to their earlier role playing. Many achieve goals similar to the spirit, if not the specifics, of their youthful dreams. But for others, the dreams and possibilities of making them come true are lost— or, at least, misplaced somewhere along the way.

The Kids' College Almanac has been written to help youngsters ages ten to fourteen keep their dreams in sight. Let us be clear: We firmly believe that childhood is a time to be treasured and enjoyed. This book is not intended to pressure youngsters to follow one particular path or another. Instead, our primary goals are to demystify college and to answer the kinds of questions young people think about at this age. Most important, we want to motivate youngsters with varying backgrounds and experiences to take advantage of the many opportunities available to them.

Throughout the book we introduce vocabulary and concepts that elementary and middle school students may have heard, but have not necessarily understood. We have provided a number of interesting facts, charts, and profiles that we hope will prove to be surprising and fun. We have also taken care to address the needs and interests of young people who face special challenges as well as those with special talents.

Youngsters can read this book from cover to cover. We hope many will. They can also read individual chapters that interest them—no special sequence is required. We think the book's most important design feature is that it can be picked up, opened to any page, read, and understood, regardless of what other pages the reader has seen. This feature enables young readers to pick and choose what interests them at any point in time.

We address topics in a direct, conversational style. We have also tried to provide a level of detail that will appeal to more sophisticated readers. By focusing on the fifty states and a wide variety of colleges, we believe our readers will see the full range of possibilities and opportunities—and learn some geography in the process!

Parents, teachers, guidance counselors, and librarians will find *The Kids' College Almanac* to be a valuable tool for answering the questions kids ask. Many parents and educators have spoken to us about their own concerns that, having gone to college many years ago, they do not feel they have the right information to advise kids about today's opportunities. We hope this book enhances their ability to motivate, encourage, and prepare young people.

One's major goals and accomplishments are rarely achieved alone. We are no exception to this rule. Our gratitude begins with our wonderful parents who proved to us that we could do whatever we wanted to if we believed in ourselves and were willing to work hard. Larry Greenfeld helped sow the seeds for this book years ago and has provided faithful support in all the years since. David Greenfeld, his friends, and the many students of all ages, stages, and places we have met throughout our careers, have taught us that young people think, plan, hope, dream, and even worry about the future— far more than is often recognized.

Our reviewers contributed valuable suggestions and guidance. In particular, we thank Jak Bestle, Rensselaer Polytechnic Institute; Jane Dingman; Dawn Mosisa, Howard Community College, Frederic Siegel, George Washington University; and Sharon Streeter. Many others contributed in important ways to the development of this book. Laura Rubin and Janelle Travers helped set the stage. Our development editor Julie Kerr provided valuable insight and enthusiastic support from the first word. Margy Kuntz and Leslie Gleason helped us develop a design that enhances the overall look of the book.

For the photographs, we are grateful to Mark Swisher; Mark Glass and Brian Speer, Colby Communications; and Randy Bengfort, Sue Probst, and Quent Kardos, Howard Community College. We also thank Jeanne Martin, Mentor Marketing and Management; Janice Jackson, Almo Music Corp; and Earl Smith, Colby College. Throughout this project, we received guidance from hundreds of college employees throughout the country. Important expertise also came from Deb Cohen, Slippery Rock University; Mariellen Baxter, University of Hartford; and Steve Cooper, National Library of Education. Additional support came from Maria Fonseca and Sioux Balamut, Sally Barhydt, Paul Bither, Diane Falk, Hank Freedman, Judith A. V. Harlan, Bill Hamill, Gregory Jbara, Wendy B. Roberts, Warren Ruud, Brian Sanderson, Adam Joshua Smargon, and Dorothy Ukeiley, among others.

Barbara adds: I am indebted to the wonderful friends, colleagues, faculty, and staff I have worked with, especially at Howard Community College. Special thanks to Jane Hemberger Brown, Jeri Kaminski, Connie Kuwamoto, Tracy Davis, Eric Lampe, Mary Ann Miller, and the Student Services workgroup. Jim Ball has encouraged me every step of the way throughout my career and laughed at all my jokes. Bob Ardinger reminded me to weave the concerns of kids facing special challenges throughout the book, not just in designated sections. I am also grateful to my other friends and colleagues, particularly Barbara Green and Joan King, who have enriched my life.

Robert adds: I would be remiss if I didn't acknowledge my teachers: Joan Keenan and Mary Lee Ruddle, Charles Bassett, Irvin "Chip" Bupp, Fred Geib, Peter Harris, Howard Koonce, Dorothy Reuman, and Robert and Helen Strider. Holly and Larry Runyan, James Streeter, and Sherman Stein all were models of integrity and commitment. My fellow singers and thespians—Paula, Naomi, Big Jim, Adele, George, and Sandi among them—provided continual support. As for Team Dounelis—Gina, Tom, George, Yia Yia, and, above all, Kathy—well, it couldn't have been done without them.

We both thank Joel and Bonni Weinstein, whose enthusiastic support and commitment made this project possible. Finally, we thank our parents again. Fran Weinstein was much more than a proud mother—she rolled up her sleeves and did whatever we needed, when we needed. Our father Gerson would be so pleased today. This book would even make up for the Red Sox not winning the World Series in his lifetime. Well, almost. . . .

B.C.G & R.A.W

And, in the very room in which he sat, there were books that could take you anywhere, and things to invent, and make, and build, and break, and all the puzzle and excitement of everything he didn't know—music to play, songs to sing, and worlds to imagine and then someday make real. His thoughts darted eagerly about as everything looked new and worth trying.

Norton Juster
The Phantom Tollbooth

1

WHAT IS COLLEGE?

College provides a bridge to the future. When you go to college, you will have the opportunity to learn new things and to build skills. You will have the opportunity to learn more about yourself and to explore careers that may be part of your future. You will also have the opportunity to make new friends and to share new experiences.

Colleges are institutions of higher education. They let you continue your education at a higher level, beyond what you learn in middle school or high school. Most colleges work in much the same way. Yet they can take many forms, as you will see. Because of these differences, you will have the opportunity to find a college that's right for you!

Types of Colleges

Many colleges can be described as liberal arts colleges. The "liberal" in liberal arts does not refer to politics. It refers to the idea that students should study a wide variety of subjects, receiving experience in many fields of study.

Some colleges are research colleges. They not only teach students, but also serve as centers for original research. When you hear or read about medical breakthroughs, you will find that many are made at research colleges and universities.

Other colleges are thought of as teaching colleges. People who teach at these colleges may conduct research, but they are especially interested in teaching. Your learning goals may influence which type of college you choose.

Colleges and Universities

College. Schooling after high school, often in four-year programs which offer bachelor degrees (Chapter 5); can be part of larger university.

University. Larger institution combining one or more colleges with other schools such as law school; usually has graduate degree programs.

Community College. Also called junior college; provides programs leading to associate degrees and professional certificates; requirements for graduation can be completed in two years; students often continue their education at four-year colleges or universities.

Agriculture and Technology College. Can either be two-year or four-year school; special emphasis may be given to agricultural programs such as farming and ranching, technological programs such as machine tooling and computer drafting, or many other areas of study.

HISTORY OF COLLEGES

Did you know that colleges have origins that date back thousands of years? Plato's Academy and Aristotle's Lyceum, established in ancient Greece in the fourth century B.C., are thought of as the first colleges. Ancient Rome, Egypt, Palestine, Babylonia, and India were centers for the study of religion, philosophy, war, and diplomacy. Two major centers for Islamic studies, located in Egypt and Morocco, are both more than one thousand years old!

Many of the major universities in Paris are located in a section frequently called the Latin Quarter. This name comes from the days when the students living there spoke only Latin or Greek as they went around to the cafes and shops.

With the birth of schools such as the University of Paris, University of Bologna, University of Salamanca, and Oxford University in the thirteenth and fourteenth centuries, medieval Europe became the next center for colleges. Law joined both religion and philosophy as an important area of study.

Medicine, science, and literature were important during the Renaissance period that followed. New colleges were established throughout Europe as well as the Americas. Asian and African nations have seen the steady growth of colleges over the past two hundred years.

The word college *comes from the Latin word* collegium, *which means society. Students would form their own societies, living and studying together, as they still do at many colleges. The word* university *comes from the union of teachers and students. Today we often interchange the words college and university. In general, however, colleges are frequently part of a larger university.*

COLLEGE IN THE UNITED STATES

The Pilgrims arrived at Plymouth Rock in 1620. Just sixteen years later, the school we know as Harvard College was founded. By the American Revolution (1776-1783), several more leading colleges had been established. Among them: the College of William and Mary, Yale University, Princeton University, Columbia University, Brown University, Rutgers (The State University of New Jersey), and Dartmouth College.

By the Civil War (1861-1865), the number had grown a lot. Most colleges founded in this period were privately funded. Although many began with ties to religious organizations, most eventually loosened or cut these ties altogether. For example, in 1693 the College of William and Mary was set up to train clergy for the Anglican Church. It then took on broader goals. It became sponsored by the Commonwealth of Virginia in 1906.

The number of colleges has continued to grow with the addition of public, private, land-grant, and community colleges. In fact, today you can choose from over 3,500 colleges and universities in the United States!

A decade after serving as the third president of the United States (1801-1809), Thomas Jefferson founded the University of Virginia. The university was set up in 1819 and opened its doors in 1825. Jefferson also played an important role in deciding what subjects would be taught at the university. Many of the original buildings, which Jefferson designed, are still being used today.

The University of Nebraska is one of the nation's oldest land-grant colleges. University Hall (right) was the university's first building. It was built on the north edge of the city of Lincoln in 1869, the same year the University of Nebraska held its first classes.

Today, over 2.5 million students attend the various state universities and land-grant colleges.

Land-Grant colleges. In 1862 and 1890, the Morrill Acts (Land-Grant Acts) led to major changes in American education. The laws gave land and money to individual states. The land and money were used to fund, support, and maintain colleges emphasizing the study of agriculture and mechanic arts (engineering). These colleges were established to provide educational opportunities and training to the working classes.

The 1890 law divided grants between colleges for white students and colleges for black students in states practicing segregation. Many historically black colleges were founded in the late 1800s with these grants.

Well before the Morrill Acts were passed, the University of North Carolina was established by the General Assembly of North Carolina in 1789 as the country's first state university. Located in Chapel Hill, the university now consists of 14 colleges and schools. With its faculty of 2,100 teachers, the University of North Carolina serves 24,000 students.

Do You Know Your State's Oldest College?

State	College or University	Year Founded
Alabama	Athens State College	1822
Alaska	Sheldon Jackson College	1878
Arizona	Arizona State University	1885
	University of Arizona	1885
Arkansas	University of the Ozarks	1834
California	Santa Clara University	1851
	University of the Pacific	1851
Colorado	University of Denver	1864
Connecticut	Yale University	1701
Delaware	University of Delaware	1743
Florida	Florida State University	1857
Georgia	University of Georgia	1785
Hawaii	University of Hawaii	1907
Idaho	Ricks College	1888
Illinois	McKendree College	1828
Indiana	Vincennes University	1801
Iowa	Loras College	1839
Kansas	Highland Community College	1858
Kentucky	Transylvania University	1780
Louisiana	Centenary College	1825
Maine	Bowdoin College	1794
Maryland	Washington College	1782
Massachusetts	Harvard University	1636
Michigan	University of Michigan	1817
Minnesota	University of Minnesota	1851
Mississippi	Mississippi College	1826
Missouri	Saint Louis University	1818
Montana	Rocky Mountain College	1878

Mount Holyoke College, first set up in 1837 in South Hadley, Massachusetts, is one of the nation's oldest colleges for women. Another leading women's college, Smith College, was founded in nearby Northampton in 1871.

Do You Know Your State's Oldest College?

State	College or University	Year Founded
Nebraska	Peru State College	1867
Nevada	University of Nevada—Reno	1874
New Hampshire	Dartmouth College	1769
New Jersey	Princeton University	1746
New Mexico	New Mexico State University	1888
New York	Columbia University	1754
North Carolina	Salem College	1772
North Dakota	Jamestown College	1883
	University of North Dakota	1883
Ohio	Ohio University	1804
Oklahoma	Northeastern State University	1846
Oregon	Willamette University	1842
Pennsylvania	University of Pennsylvania	1740
Rhode Island	Brown University	1764
South Carolina	College of Charleston	1770
South Dakota	Augustana College	1860
Tennessee	Tusculum College	1794
Texas	Southwestern University	1840
Utah	University of Utah	1850
Vermont	Castleton State College	1787
Virginia	College of William and Mary	1693
Washington	Whitman College	1859
West Virginia	Marshall University	1837
	West Liberty State College	1837
Wisconsin	Beloit College	1846
	Carroll College	1846
Wyoming	University of Wyoming	1886
District of Columbia	Georgetown University	1789

In 1779, the University of Pennsylvania received its fourth name! Benjamin Franklin founded it as the Charity School in 1740. In 1750, it became the Academy of Philadelphia and then the College of Pennsylvania in 1755.

Community and junior colleges. Some two-year colleges have been around since the nineteenth century. Vincennes University in Indiana, founded in 1801, is one of the oldest two-year colleges in the United States. After World War II, there was a great demand for local colleges. These colleges could respond to the educational and training needs of the community. They could also meet the needs of people who could not commit to four years of full-time college. Soldiers returning from war, the growth of the suburbs, and the entrance of more women into the workforce were factors that led to the founding of community colleges across the United States.

In many cases, the two years you spend at a community college are equivalent to the first two years you would spend at a four-year college.

For some people, community colleges provide a stepping stone to four-year colleges. They offer lower costs, closeness to home, and more personal instruction. For many, they offer opportunities to further their education while managing a job or family resonsibilities. For others still, community colleges provide the chance to learn specific job skills, prepare for a career, or take a course for pleasure.

Like many community colleges, Flathead Valley Community College in northwestern Montana got its start in the 1960s. Flathead Valley (right) is an example of a college that brings educational opportunities to students who live in less populated rural areas.

And Don't Forget These Older Colleges . . .

State	College or University	Year Founded
Pennsylvania	Moravian College	1742
Virginia	Washington and Lee University	1749
New Jersey	Rutgers	1764
Pennsylvania	Dickinson College	1773
Virginia	Hampden-Sydney College	1776
Pennsylvania	Washington and Jefferson College	1781
Maryland	Saint John's College	1784
North Carolina	Louisburg College	1787
Pennsylvania	Franklin and Marshall College	1787
Pennsylvania	University of Pittsburgh	1787
Pennsylvania	York College	1787
North Carolina	University of North Carolina	1789
Vermont	University of Vermont	1791
Massachusetts	Williams College	1793
Tennessee	University of Tennessee	1794
New York	Union College	1795
New York	Hartwick College	1797
Kentucky	University of Louisville	1798

Technology colleges. Passage of the Land-Grant Acts led to the founding of many colleges that provide education in technology, architecture, engineering, and agriculture. In addition, many other fine schools specializing in technology have been established through the years.

One of the first was Rensselaer Polytechnic Institute (RPI), founded in 1824 in Troy, New York. Other leading technology colleges include Case Western Reserve University (1826), Cooper Union (1859), Massachusetts Institute of Technology (1861), Pratt Institute (1887), California Institute of Technology (1891), and Carnegie Mellon University (1900).

Statewide systems. Many states link a variety of colleges and universities together in a statewide system. For example, the State University of New York (SUNY) includes four university centers, thirteen state university colleges, six technology colleges, and thirty community colleges. It also includes several health science centers and other specialized colleges. About 400,000 students are enrolled at the various SUNY colleges. Of these, about half attend one of the community colleges located throughout the state.

Adirondack Community College (ACC), located in upstate New York, is one of many community colleges in the SUNY system. Like many community colleges, ACC (right) has arrangements for many of its students to continue their education at four-year colleges and universities.

SUNY-Buffalo is a major research institution that is one of four university centers in the SUNY system. The South Campus (right) is near a residential section of Buffalo. It houses most of the university's health sciences programs. It can be easily reached by public transportation.

State University of New York (SUNY)

University Centers

Albany
Binghamton
Buffalo
Stony Brook

State University Colleges

Brockport
Buffalo
Cortland
Empire State College
Fredonia
Geneseo
New Paltz
Old Westbury
Oneonta
Oswego
Plattsburgh
Potsdam
Purchase

Technology Colleges

Alfred
Canton
Cobleskill
Delhi
Farmingdale
Morrisville

Additional Colleges

Environmental Science and Forestry
Maritime College
College of Optometry
Institute of Technology—Utica/Rome

Community Colleges

Adirondack
Broome
Cayuga County
Clinton
Columbia-Greene
Corning
Dutchess
Erie
Fashion Institute of Technology
Finger Lakes
Fulton-Montgomery
Genesee
Herkimer County
Hudson Valley
Jamestown
Jefferson
Mohawk Valley
Monroe
Nassau
Niagara County
North Country
Onondaga
Orange County
Rockland
Schenectady County
Suffolk County
Sullivan County
Tompkins-Cortland
Ulster County
Westchester

Health Science Centers

Brooklyn
Buffalo
Stony Brook
Syracuse

WHAT IS AFFILIATION?

Affiliation refers to ways we organize colleges and their students into groups. For instance, we can look at a college's relationship with its founders (e.g., a religious group). We can also look at whether men, women, or both men and women attend a certain college.

College Affiliations

Public vs. Private. Public colleges: supported by taxpayers; under the supervision of federal, state, or local governments; less expensive for local students. Private colleges: independent; supported by private funds; under much less government supervision; usually cost more to attend.

Religion. Many colleges affiliated with religious groups; in some cases, group has much say about how the college is run; other times, affiliation is looser; students often don't have to belong to the specific religious group in order to attend.

Gender. Some colleges accept only male students or female students; coeducational (co-ed) colleges accept both female and male students; many colleges have become coeducational to attract more students.

Race and Ethnicity. Strong ties to particular racial or ethnic groups; historically and predominantly black colleges accept mostly African-American students, though others may attend; many established at a time when black students were denied opportunity to study at other colleges.

Military. Train students for careers in the military; can be under federal or state supervision; many other colleges offer ROTC (Reserve Officer Training Corps) programs as part of overall studies.

Proprietary. Often run by companies for profit; provide strong career training; fields include secretarial, business, computer, electronics, technical, and culinary (cooking) fields.

Historically/Predominantly Black Colleges

State	College or University	Year Founded
Alabama	Alabama State University	1874
Alabama	Tuskegee University	1881
Arkansas	Philander Smith College	1877
Delaware	Delaware State College	1891
Florida	Florida A & M University	1887
Georgia	Morehouse College	1867
Georgia	Spelman College	1881
Louisiana	Grambling State University	1901
Maryland	Morgan State University	1867
Mississippi	Alcorn State University	1871
Mississippi	Jackson State University	1877
North Carolina	Fayetteville State University	1867
Ohio	Central State University	1887
South Carolina	South Carolina State College	1896
Tennessee	Fisk University	1866
Tennessee	LeMoyne-Owen College	1862
Texas	Prairie View A & M University	1876
Texas	Texas Southern University	1947
Virginia	Hampton University	1868
Virginia	Norfolk State University	1935
District of Columbia	Howard University	1867

Many colleges that once admitted only male or female students have since become coeducational. For instance, Amherst College in Massachusetts was founded in 1821, but did not become fully coeducational until 1976.

Colleges with the name Wesleyan in them, such as Ohio Wesleyan University, are (or once were) affiliated with the United Methodist Church. The name comes from John Wesley, the founder of Methodism.

☞ HOW DOES A COLLEGE WORK?

In many ways, you can think of a college as a business. A college offers a product and services to its customers. In this case, the product is a good education. The customers are the students.

Behind the scenes are the various pieces that help the college make its product available to students. The administration is the management team of the college. The faculty bring the product directly to the students. You can look at classrooms, labs, and libraries as the factories where the education is produced. College services make sure that everything runs smoothly and that students are able to take full advantage of their education. The alumni and community, including government and local businesses, provide support that help make the college successful.

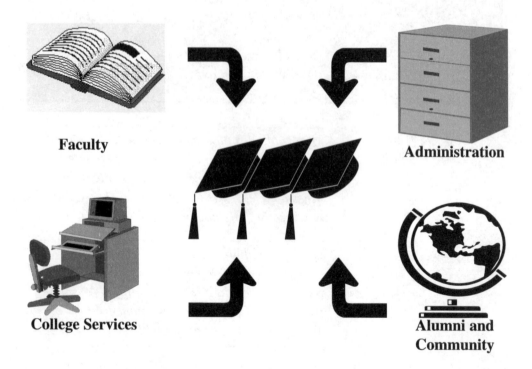

Faculty

Administration

College Services

Alumni and Community

Students who have not yet graduated from college are undergraduates. Students who have graduated from college and are studying at an advanced level are graduate students.

What is the student body? The name given to all the students as a whole is the student body. At a four-year college, students can be divided into four groups, just as they are in high school. The first-year students are freshmen and second-year students are sophomores. Students in their third year are juniors. Those in their fourth or final year are seniors. Juniors and seniors are also referred to as upperclassmen.

What does the administration do? You may have heard about the president's administration—the people who run the United States government. In a similar way, a college's administration handles both the daily running of the college and its long-term planning. The exact way colleges are set up may vary somewhat from one college to another.

Who Runs a College?

Board of Trustees. Sometimes called the Board of Directors; a group of people who hire and supervise a college's president and, sometimes, other key employees; determine tuition (college costs); approve new buildings, new academic programs, and major spending; establish broad goals for the college.

President. Hires and manages the people who run major portions of the college; works closely with the board of trustees on important issues affecting the college's future; raises money for the college from businesses, alumni, the community, and other sources.

Deans. Also called vice-presidents; responsible for major portions of the college; Dean of Faculty (Dean of Instruction) hires and oversees the teachers and the subjects that are taught; Dean of Students oversees programs that help students, such as counseling, athletics, and housing; also oversees important policies and procedures that affect students, such as the honor code (policies regarding honesty and conduct).

Teaching assistants, also called "TAs," help professors who teach large classes. TAs often meet with students in smaller study groups. They sometimes teach their own classes.

Who are the faculty? The people who teach at colleges are the faculty. Professors are full-time teachers who have a long-term relationship at the college. Professors may be given tenure if they meet teaching, research, or publishing require-ments set by the college. Tenure is a guarantee of job security at the college.

Depending on how long they have been teaching at the college, professors might be full professors, associate professors, or assistant professors. When professors retire, they are often awarded the title *professor emeritus*. Sometimes they still teach an occasional class at the college.

Instructors are usually entry-level teachers. Some-times they fill in for professors who are on leave. Other times, the instructors are still finishing their advanced studies at another university. Lecturers and adjunct (part-time) instructors often teach one or two classes for the college. Graduate assistants and teaching assistants are graduate students who also help teach introductory courses. Sometimes they help professors in other ways, for instance, by grading papers and tests. They spend most of their time, however, on their own studies.

What are college services? Every college has a group of people who help you get the most out of your time at college. Some, like advisors and counselors, work directly with students. Others work more behind the scenes to help keep things running smoothly. We'll come back to many of them again later in the book. Meanwhile, some of the major services they offer are described on the following page.

College Services

Admissions. Informs students about the college; assists students who are applying to the college; determines who is accepted to attend.

Financial Aid. Helps qualified students get federal and state financial aid; distributes scholarships, grants, and loans to qualified students; also helps coordinate college job programs that enable students to work at the college.

Registration. Registers students for their classes; helps students change their schedules; maintains student records, including grades; provides official information to students about their transcripts (their college record), often needed when applying for graduate school or jobs.

Testing and Placement. Evaluates students' abilities, usually in math and English; determines which classes students are ready to take; helps students find review classes to brush up on needed skills.

Counseling and Advising. Helps students select their classes and plan their schedules; helps students explore career options; also assists with personal concerns, as well as study and organizational skills.

Special Services. Works with students who have physical handicaps or learning disabilities such as dyslexia; also works with students who have other individual needs.

Student Center and Student Activities. Works with Student Government Association; provides recreational activities on and off campus; organizes special student activities like guest lectures and concerts; may oversee student newspaper and other publications; works with clubs to arrange meeting space or funding.

Health Center. Also called the infirmary; provides medical care.

Other Offices. Buildings and grounds maintains college facilities and landscaping; security provides a safe environment; food service oversees dining halls, meals, and special events.

Who are the alumni? People who have already graduated from a particular college are the alumni of that college. Alumni are an important resource. They contribute money that helps keep your costs down. They help recruit and interview students who are still deciding where to go. You often have the chance to meet alumni at school fairs and other special events. Alumni advise the administration about long-term policies for the college. They are also an important part of a college's school spirit.

Many colleges open their events and facilities to local residents. Art museum tours, concerts, and use of athletic facilities, such as the swimming pool or ice skating arena, help to build a bond between the college and the community.

How important is the community? In many ways, the most important relationship that any college has is with the people and businesses in the community where it is located. Faculty and students live in the community. Many alumni also live in the community. Local businesses often hire students from a nearby college, both while they are still students and after they graduate. Local businesses may also help fund special programs at the college. Communities that offer lots of places to go and a lot of things to do help colleges attract students.

Comparing Your School with College

Middle or High School	College or University
School Board	Board of Trustees
Principal	President
Vice-Principal	Deans/Vice-Presidents
Teacher	Professor
Guidance Counselor	Career Counselor
Guidance Counselor	Advisor
Nurse's Office	Infirmary
Library/Media Center	Learning Resource Center

2 WHY SHOULD I THINK ABOUT COLLEGE?

Some kids have always known that college is in their future. Is this true for you?

Or are you someone who has never thought much about college? Maybe you think that you're not smart enough, that you could never afford college, or that going to college wouldn't be very useful. Perhaps none of your friends are thinking about college—so why should you?

Your decisions about college are among the most important ones you will ever make. And to make these decisions, you will need information.

LEARNING OPPORTUNITIES

So far, your education has focused on learning many different skills—reading, writing, and math, among many others. You have studied different subjects. However, you haven't yet had a great deal of choice about what subjects you study or when you take them. For the most part, you and your classmates have studied the same things. While you may have studied them at different levels, the subjects were still the same.

This pattern begins to change in high school. At that time, you have more choices about what to take. You begin to learn about the subjects and careers that really interest you.

College provides even more choices. You can learn practical skills, such as how to listen to a patient's heart beat or the mechanics of editing a film. You can also study at a broader level, learning how the heart functions in a person's body or how various styles of editing affect the way that audiences react to different movies.

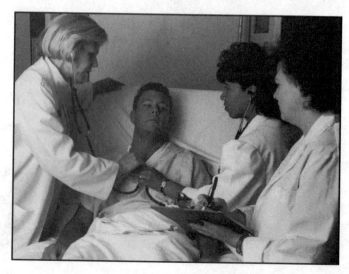

You can also choose certain courses just because they're fun, different, or interesting—no matter whether they are or are not related to your major area of study or to the work you plan to do.

College may prepare you for your chosen career. But it definitely prepares you for a lifetime of learning at work, in school, or in the community. You have, in fact, the chance to become an expert learner.

In many ways, the most important skill you can learn at college is how to learn. If you master this skill, then you can succeed throughout life. After all, you may find at some point in your life that you want to—or have to—make changes. In the computerized and high technology world in which we live, careers change and older skills can go out of date.

But by becoming a lifelong learner, you can and will have the confidence and ability to learn what you need and want to learn throughout the rest of your life!

CAREER OPPORTUNITIES

College isn't only about studying specific subjects. At college you also learn more about yourself and what interests you. And you learn what doors of opportunity are waiting to be opened by someone just like you.

What would you like to do when you grow up? Don't be surprised if you are not sure yet what you want to do or what opportunities are available to you. Actually, most kids aren't sure. That includes college kids too. Fortunately, learning about your career opportunities is an area where college can be of great help to you.

More important than knowing exactly what you want to be is understanding some basic things about careers. For instance, some careers require a college education, though others do not. If you want to be a nurse, you *must* complete college. However, running your own business may not require a college education, although the courses you take can improve your chances for success.

For many careers, college is just the beginning. To be a lawyer, you must first go to college and then to law school. You can enter other careers with different levels of education. And various jobs within career fields may require different amounts of education.

For example, to be a school teacher, you must be a college graduate. Many school teachers must continue their studies after college. To be a principal or a college professor, however, you must have advanced studies beyond college.

The amount of education you need is not the only thing that differs among careers. Some careers, such as those in computer science and engineering, require specific skills. In turn, you need to take specific courses to develop these skills.

Other careers are less specific. You can enter them with a broader range of courses and skills. For example, if you go into sales, you might have a background in business, economics, liberal arts, or communications.

The images we have of different careers are not always accurate. We often get our sense from the movies, television, or the news. Would it surprise you to know that the FBI is especially interested in hiring people who have studied accounting?

In short: Learning what people in a career really do and what educational training they have is very important for planning your future.

Fast-Growing Occupations

Occupation	Projected Increase in Number of Jobs 1992-2005
Home health aides	479,000
Child care workers	450,000
*Special education teachers	267,000
*Human services	256,000
*Computer engineers and scientists	236,000
Correction officers	197,000
*Radiologic technologists/technicians	102,000
*Physical therapists	79,000

These careers require a college education.

How can I find out more about careers? Information about jobs that people do is all around us. Yet we usually miss it. For example, have you ever thought of asking your doctor questions such as: Why did you become a doctor? What do you have to do to become a doctor? Where did you go to school? How did you choose which kind of doctor to be? What do you like best about your job? What do you like least?

Most of us never ask these kinds of questions. But why not? Most people enjoy talking about themselves and will gladly give you answers.

People all around you—family, friends, parents of classmates, teachers, neighbors—can help you learn more about careers. Don't be afraid to pose hard questions. And understand that the people you ask won't be able to give you magic answers that decide for you. However, the answers you get will help you find your own direction.

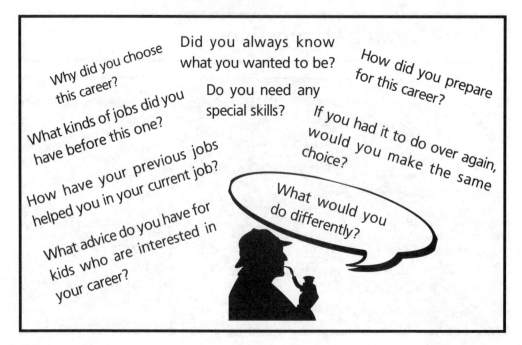

Career days. Your school probably offers many opportunities to learn more about careers. Your school may even have a career day every year. Career days are special days when people from your community come to your school and share information about their jobs.

The U.S. Department of Labor publishes two important sources of information about jobs. The Dictionary of Occupational Titles *lists almost all possible jobs—over 25,000! And* The Occupational Outlook Handbook *describes types of careers, specific jobs, and information about the training needed for these jobs. The reference librarian at your school can help you find these resources.*

Many people have careers that you would quickly think of if you were asked to make up a list of jobs—lawyer, doctor, police officer, teacher, and so forth. Others have careers you may not think of quite so quickly—editor, college admissions counselor, criminologist, microbiologist, product manager, plant supervisor, or surveyor.

If you go to a career day, talk to as many people as you can. Listen closely and ask questions. Some people have always known what they want to do. Others have made choices based on experiences and opportunities that came along. People often go in different directions than they had expected.

Some people want to be their own boss. Some prefer working for others, letting them worry about running the company. Some people want to travel. Others want to stay closer to home. Some people want to do a job that has little to do with their personal hobbies. Others want to combine those interests with their job.

When Paul Bither went to college, he planned to study French. During his freshman year, his mother suffered a serious eye injury. This experience led Paul toward the sciences—and exploring eye care. After college, he went to optometry school. He is now an optometrist and specializes in patients with low vision.

What are career centers? Every college has an office that provides information and advice about careers. At these career development or career counseling centers you can find information about careers through books, videos, tapes, computer programs, and other sources.

These centers help you explore different career paths. You can learn about the different jobs that are available in various fields. You can also learn about the kind of training needed to succeed.

Career testing and counseling can help you find out things about yourself that might be important when you choose a career. These services help you identify your interests and strengths. Through a combination of conversations, surveys, and tests, a career counselor can help you learn more about your personal likes, dislikes, and skills, and how these compare with the likes, dislikes, and skills of people who work in different jobs.

Did you ever wonder why some products—for instance, certain brands of sneakers or jeans—are more popular than others? The way in which these products are marketed is often the key to their success.

For example, you might find you have an interest in marketing—the way products are brought to the marketplace. However, you might be unsure where to start. Marketing is a broad field with lots of different opportunities in areas such as advertising, sales, and research.

A career counselor can help you find a good fit. Suppose you are an outgoing person who enjoys meeting new people. You may prefer to go into sales. If you are a creative or artistic person who is clever with words and new ideas, advertising may be a better choice for you. If you are shy, but like to write and work with numbers, then research might be your best bet.

Many job placement offices offer students workshops on writing resumes, interview skills, and searching for jobs. At many colleges, students have the opportunity to interview for jobs with hundreds of businesses, government agencies, and other organizations that come to recruit students.

What is job placement? Most career centers have a job placement office. This office invites employers to the college to interview students. Most companies that talk to students prefer to hire those who are ready to graduate. But, in some cases, companies hire students for the summer. In this way the companies can see if the student is someone they would want to hire for full-time work after college. The job placement office can not guarantee you will find work with firms that come to the college. It simply creates opportunities for you to meet with different companies.

Is college the only way to prepare for a career? In some cases, college *is* the only way. But for some careers, your options include vocational and proprietary schools, technical institutes, and other specialized programs. These schools often focus on specialized areas: electronics, culinary arts, plumbing, cosmetology, and so forth.

Remember: No one can take education and skills away from you. The more you have, the better off you will be!

Careers and College Education

Requiring at Least Two Years of College

Air traffic controller
Computer programmer
Computer technician
Food service manager
Graphic artist
Insurance claims representative

Nurse
Paralegal
Radiology technologist
Respiratory therapist
Telecommunications technican
Wildlife manager

Requiring at Least Four Years of College

Accountant
Computer engineer
Financial services representative
Interior designer
Landscape architect
Mechanical engineer

Meteorologist
Occupational therapist
Personnel manager
Public relations manager
Statistician
Teacher

Requiring more than Four Years of College

Architect
Athletic trainer
Clinical social worker
Dentist
Doctor
Guidance counselor
Judge

Lawyer
Librarian
Minister, priest, or rabbi
Pharmacist
Physical therapist
Principal
Professor

Many occupations require you to be licensed by the state—to go through a formal process in which the state grants you permission to work in the field. Licenses may be required in such diverse fields as teaching, social work, law, plumbing, real estate appraisal, medicine, and counseling.

Career Opportunities at College

You can prepare for many of these careers at numerous colleges across the country. This list simply provides examples of the range of careers that await you and some examples of colleges where you can prepare for these careers.

Career	Example of a College Offering this Career Program
Archaeologist	Cornell University (NY)
Architect	Massachusetts Inst. of Technology
Astronomer	University of Arizona
Court reporter	University of Mississippi
Dance therapist	Goucher College (MD)
Earthquake engineer	University of California—Berkeley
Farmer	Texas A & M University
Fire protection engineer	Oklahoma State University
Flight trainer	Embry-Riddle Aeronautical U. (FL)
Forest ranger	Oregon State University
Hotel manager	University of Nevada—Las Vegas
Interior designer	O'More College of Design (TN)
Journalist	Northwestern University (IL)
Librarian	University of Chicago (IL)
Marine biologist	Univ. of California—Santa Barbara
Medical illustrator	Rochester Inst. of Technology (NY)
Miner	Colorado School of Mines
Opera singer	Indiana University
Pharmacist	Philadelphia Coll. of Pharmacy (PA)
Social worker	Columbia University (NY)
Theater designer	Carnegie Mellon University (PA)
Veterinarian	University of Maryland

Two-year colleges offer a wide range of career programs. At Tarrant County Junior College in Texas, your choices include automotive collision repair, dental hygiene, fashion merchandising, interpreting for the deaf, postal service administration, real estate, small engine repair, and welding technology.

ARTISTIC AND ATHLETIC OPPORTUNITIES

Colleges provide students with opportunities to develop acting, directing, musical, and artistic skills. In most cases, students simply enjoy these experiences and follow up on them through church and local choirs, community theater, and personal relaxation. Some students choose professional careers in the arts. If you are interested in the arts as a career, you should look for colleges that offer special programs in your area of interest.

Several colleges focus primarily on the performing arts. Among them are Berklee College of Music, the American Academy of Dramatic Arts, the Conservatory of Music at Oberlin College, and the Hartt School at the University of Hartford.

Other colleges emphasize the visual arts. These include the Art Academy of Cincinnati, Rhode Island School of Design, Maryland Institute—College of Art, and San Francisco Art Institute.

Greg Jbara studied communications and physics at the University of Michigan. When he realized acting was where his talents were, he left Michigan, trained more, and went to The Juilliard School. Since graduating, Greg has moved from national touring companies to off-Broadway shows to featured roles in hit Broadway shows such as Damn Yankees *and* Victor/Victoria. *Greg highly recommends a college education. He notes: Few people in this world are prepared to make choices about careers right out of high school. Remember, you can always change schools or career options or hair color! You always have the option to change your course in life.*

Students headed for athletic careers, especially in sports such as basketball, football, and track and field, use their college years to develop their skills. Top athletes in other fields such as swimming, gymnastics, and wrestling, as well as hockey, baseball, and tennis, often compete at the college level. College provides opportunities as well for people who are interested in coaching, training, sports therapy, and sports psychology.

Only a small number of college athletes are able to move to the professional ranks successfully. Be realistic about your abilities. Always prepare for a career other than professional athlete.

For most students, athletics simply enriches their college years. Even if you do not play on one of the school's official teams, you can participate in a wide range of sports activities.

Most colleges have intramural sports. Students form teams and play other teams from within the college. Intramural teams are usually available to anyone who wants to play. Also, many colleges have excellent facilities that let all students play racquetball or squash, lift weights, swim, run track, and play basketball.

In 1969, Mike Reid was one of the best college football players in the country. As a defensive tackle for Penn State's undefeated football team, he won the Outland Trophy for Best Interior Lineman and the Maxwell Award for the Nation's Outstanding Player. He then played several years in the National Football League with the Cincinnati Bengals, winning awards such as Rookie of the Year. While at Penn State, Mike prepared for life after football by studying music. Eventually he switched to a career in music. Today, he is a successful composer, with hit songs for artists such as Bonnie Raitt. He has also expanded his range to include modern dance scores and opera.

LIFE OPPORTUNITIES

When you think about college, you may think first about studying and preparing for a career. But college also enriches your personal life. It helps you make important transitions in your life.

Living independently. Like many students, you may find that your first real opportunity to live away from your parents and family comes when you go to college. You will have to take greater personal responsibility on a day-to-day basis.

For example, right now you may be used to being asked every day if you've finished your homework. Maybe you are not allowed to do some things—watch TV, play computer games, talk on the phone—until your homework is done.

 When you go to college, you probably won't be asked about homework all the time. You won't be told when during the day you must do it. But while you might like this freedom, you might find that being asked about homework helped you stay on track. Now you will have to motivate yourself to succeed. You will have to set your own schedule.

For every freedom that you gain, you also gain a responsibility. Learning to balance these two— freedom and responsibility—is just one part of college. But it is a very important life skill.

You'll find lots of support at college for making this transition. You will know when assignments are due. Professors will usually tell you when you will have exams. And lots of college services will be nearby, ready to help you organize your time.

Establishing goals. You don't have to be sure about what you want to do after college in order to start college. But college gives you the chance to think about what is important to you and what you would like your life to be like.

Starting college is like starting a new year when you make resolutions. Goals vary. Your list of goals may include preparing for a career, getting good grades, trying new activities, learning new skills, or making new friends. Setting goals will help you get more out of the college experience.

Meeting a wide range of people. When you go to college, you have the chance to meet people with backgrounds different from your own. Your classmates may be people from other parts of the state or country. They may be from other parts of the world. Their cultural and religious background may be very different from yours.

You will meet people of all ages with various points of view. Your classmates and teachers will have experiences different from yours. Therefore, you will be exposed to new ideas, viewpoints, and lifestyles.

You will want to think carefully about how other people's perspectives fit with your own opinions, goals, and values. You will be able to use this experience to learn more about yourself.

And you will make new friends. Some of the friends you make in college will become lifelong friends. Others may become important to you in other ways, for example, helping you find a job later in life.

Exploring new opportunities. Perhaps the most exciting part of college is the chance to try new experiences. You can take some courses simply for enjoyment or to satisfy your curiosity. You can try a new sport—perhaps rugby or lacrosse—or a recreational activity that may never have been available to you before.

You may be able to perform in a play, work on a newspaper, or join student government. You may be able to get involved in the college community, maybe coordinating a food drive, helping build housing for the homeless, organizing a rally, or raising money for charity.

You will have the opportunity to listen to and meet artists, journalists, political leaders, researchers, and others who visit the college. Some of the people whom you meet may be able to offer you advice about careers, maybe even a job! You may have the chance to travel, studying in other parts of the country or the world. Every day of college will provide new opportunities that will help you grow in new and exciting ways!

3 WHO GOES TO COLLEGE?

Two hundred years ago, the typical college student in the United States was a young, white man. Women and students of color were rarely found at college. It was not really until the 1830s that changes began to take place. For instance, when Oberlin College in Ohio was founded in 1835, the trustees expressed a clear interest in educating students of color. And in 1841, the first three women in the United States to receive A.B. degrees (see Chapter 5) graduated from Oberlin.

How times have changed! Today anyone who wants to go to college has the opportunity to go. Perhaps before too long, you'll join the ranks!

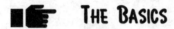 ## THE BASICS

If you decide to attend college someday, you will not be alone. Did you know that every year more than 14 million students attend college?

Four-year and two-year students. Enrollment in two-year colleges has skyrocketed in the past forty years. Today about 40 percent of all college students attend community colleges.

Four-Year and Two-Year Students
1991-1992

Two-year students
39.5%

Four-year students
60.5%

Some colleges require all freshmen to live in college-run housing. Then after the first year, students have more choice about where they live. Many believe that first-year students have enough of an adjustment to make without adding on the responsibility of managing a home.

Residential students and commuters. At some colleges, the majority of students live in housing owned and operated by the college. This is true especially at smaller colleges that require you to attend full-time. Living at the college with other students is considered an important part of the college experience.

Other colleges offer no college-run housing. This is most often the case at two-year colleges. At these colleges, students live at home or on their own. They must travel (commute) to and from college each day.

Full-time and part-time students. Students who go to a four-year college on a full-time basis can usually graduate in four years. Similarly, students who go to a two-year college on a full-time basis can graduate in two years.

An increasing number of programs, for instance, in fields such as engineering and architecture, are five-year programs.

Many people cannot attend college full time. They may have other commitments such as holding down a job or taking care of their family. For some, money is an issue. Many students simply prefer to take one or two courses at a time rather than a full load of classes. Most colleges, though not all, allow you to attend part time. If this is the option you prefer, double check that any colleges of interest to you will let you attend part time.

Day and evening students. Many colleges give you lots of choices about when to take your classes. Community colleges in particular have developed their schedules to meet the needs of the working student. Students can attend evening classes or even classes on weekends. Some classes meet only once a week. Many colleges also offer early morning classes you can take before work.

Scottsdale Community College (SCC) in Arizona, like many other colleges, offers courses at a variety of times throughout the day. For example, you can take an English composition class as early as 7:30 a.m. For students who can only attend classes at night, SCC offers the same course starting as late as 7:15 p.m.

Age. You may have heard others say that learning is a lifelong commitment. When we look at the ages of college students in the 1990s, we can see this idea in action.

Today's college students come from all age groups. The majority of full-time students are under 24 years old. But the majority of part-time students are older than 24.

Older students, many of whom have already been to college, take college courses for a variety of reasons. Changes in technology require workers to update their knowledge. Students hoping to change careers need new information and skills. Still others find pleasure in taking courses they never had the chance to take before, or that were not available.

Community colleges have traditionally served more women than men.

Female and male students. One of the biggest changes in recent years is the number of women who attend college. In the early 1950s, about twice as many men attended college as women. By the 1970s, the women were catching up in numbers. Now, women outpace the men, with about 1.5 million more women attending college than men.

Male and Female Enrollment in College		
Year	Male Students	Female Students
1955	1,733,184	919,850
1965	3,630,020	2,290,844
1970	5,043,642	3,537,245
1975	6,148,997	5,035,882
1980	5,874,374	6,222,521
1985	5,818,450	6,428,605
1990	6,283,909	7,534,728

Women and Men at U.S. Colleges

College or University	Women*	Men*
Alabama State University	2,573	2,017
Pima Community College (AZ)	15,450	12,510
University of San Francisco (CA)	2,671	1,648
Colorado School of Mines	542	1,665
U.S. Coast Guard Academy (CT)	179	727
Florida State University	12,069	10,133
Spelman College (GA)	1,976	0
De Paul University (IL)	6,601	4,183
Indiana University—Bloomington	14,247	11,935
Kirkwood Community College (IA)	5,612	4,140
Kansas State University	7,845	9,147
Bates College (ME)	800	762
United States Naval Academy (MD)	539	3,555
Massachusetts Institute of Technology	1,604	2,868
University of Michigan	11,185	12,053
University of Mississippi	4,038	3,812
Dana College (NE)	357	293
Colby-Sawyer College (NH)	449	226
Trenton State College (NJ)	3,905	2,368
Westchester Community College (NY)	6,433	4,914
Duke University (NC)	2,867	3,277
Ohio State University at Columbus	16,990	19,176
Reed College (OR)	635	623
Lehigh University (PA)	1,632	2,774
Rhode Island School of Design	1,023	837
Furman University (SC)	1,315	1,133
University of South Dakota	3,012	2,637
Vanderbilt University (TN)	2,734	3,126
Tarrant County Junior College (TX)	15,114	11,728
Radford University (VA)	4,651	3,495
Shoreline Community College (WA)	4,385	3,129
Marquette University (WI)	3,970	3,721

*Number of full-time and part-time undergraduate students, fall 1994

Who Went Where to College?

Graduate	College
Jim Abbott *(athlete, baseball)*	University of Michigan
Daniel Akaka *(senator)*	University of Hawaii
Madeleine Albright *(U.N. ambassador)*	Wellesley College *(MA)*
Ronald Allen *(head of Delta Airlines)*	Georgia Inst. of Technology
Christine Amanpour *(CNN news reporter)*	University of Rhode Island
Ruth Bader Ginsburg *(Supreme Court)*	Cornell University *(NY)*
Erma Bombeck *(columnist)*	University of Dayton *(OH)*
Tom Brokaw *(news anchor)*	University of South Dakota
Garth Brooks *(country music singer)*	Oklahoma State University
Joyce Brothers *(psychologist)*	Cornell University *(NY)*
Ken Burns *(filmmaker, historian)*	Hampshire College *(MA)*
Helen Gurley Brown *(editor, Cosmopolitan)*	Woodbury University *(CA)*
Ben Nighthorse Campbell *(senator)*	San Jose State Univ. *(CA)*
Mary Chapin Carpenter *(singer)*	Brown University *(RI)*
Johnny Carson *(entertainer)*	University of Nebraska
Dick Cheney *(former secretary of defense)*	University of Wyoming
Connie Chung *(television journalist)*	University of Maryland
Tom Clancy *(writer)*	Loyola College *(MD)*
Hillary Rodham Clinton *(first lady, lawyer)*	Wellesley College *(MA)*
Glenn Close *(actress)*	Coll. of Wm. and Mary *(VA)*
Johnnetta Cole *(president, Spelman College)*	Oberlin College *(OH)*
Beth Daniel *(athlete, golf)*	Furman University *(SC)*
Elizabeth Dole *(head of Red Cross)*	Duke University *(NC)*
Robert Dole *(senator)*	Washburn University *(KS)*
Pete Domenici *(senator)*	University of New Mexico
Michael Eisner *(head of Walt Disney Co.)*	Denison University *(OH)*

Many alumni offer help to the colleges from which they have graduated. For example, prominent television news anchor and journalist Walter Cronkite graduated from Arizona State University (ASU). More recently he helped establish the Walter Cronkite School of Journalism and Telecommunication at ASU.

Who Went Where to College?

Graduate	College
Gloria Estefan *(singer)*	University of Miami *(FL)*
Dianne Feinstein *(senator)*	Stanford University *(CA)*
Jodie Foster *(actress, director, producer)*	Yale University *(CT)*
Louis Freeh *(director of the FBI)*	Rutgers *(NJ)*
Charlayne Hunter-Gault *(TV journalist)*	University of Georgia
Louis Gerstner *(head of IBM)*	Dartmouth College *(NH)*
Doris Kearns Goodwin *(historian, writer)*	Colby College *(ME)*
Billy Graham *(evangelist)*	Wheaton College *(IL)*
Rev. Bill Gray *(United Negro College Fund)*	Franklin and Marshall Coll. *(PA)*
Jeff Greenfield *(news analyst)*	University of Wisconsin
John Grisham *(writer)*	Mississippi State University
Herbie Hancock *(jazz musician)*	Grinnell College *(IA)*
Orrin Hatch *(senator)*	Brigham Young Univ. *(UT)*
Grant Hill *(athlete, basketball)*	Duke University *(NC)*
S.E. Hinton *(writer)*	University of Tulsa *(OK)*
Molly Ivins *(columnist)*	Smith College *(MA)*
James Ivory *(film director)*	University of Oregon
Bo Jackson *(athlete, football, baseball)*	Auburn University *(AL)*
Jesse Jackson *(civil rights leader)*	N.C. Ag & Tech State Univ.
Steven Jobs *(cofounder, Apple Computer)*	Reed College *(OR)*
Kathy Johnson *(Olympic medalist, gymnast)*	Centenary College *(LA)*
Nancy Johnson *(congresswoman)*	Radcliffe College *(MA)*
Jerry Jones *(owner, Dallas Cowboys)*	University of Arkansas
Quincy Jones *(musician, producer)*	Berklee Coll. of Music *(MA)*
Jackie Joyner-Kersee *(heptathlon champion)*	UCLA *(CA)*
Coretta Scott King *(civil rights leader)*	Antioch College *(OH)*

Two stars of 1960s television spy series later earned doctorate degrees (see Chapter 5). Robert Vaughn of The Man From U.N.C.L.E. *earned his doctorate from the University of Southern California. Bill Cosby of* I Spy *(and later* The Cosby Show*) earned his doctorate from the University of Massachusetts.*

Who Went Where to College?

Graduate	College
Jeanne Kirkpatrick *(ambassador)*	Stephens College *(MO)*
Murray Lender *(founder, Lender's Bagels)*	Quinnipiac College *(CT)*
John Lewis *(congressman)*	Fisk University *(TN)*
Maya Lin *(architect)*	Yale University *(CT)*
Yo-Yo Ma *(cellist)*	Harvard University *(MA)*
David Mamet *(playwright)*	Goddard College *(VT)*
J. Willard Marriott *(business, hotels)*	University of Utah
Mary Matalin *(political analyst)*	Western Illinois University
Robert Matsui *(congressman)*	U. of California—Berkeley
Kathy Mattea *(country music singer)*	West Virginia University
Cynthia McKinney *(congresswoman)*	Univ. of Southern California
Terrence McNally *(playwright)*	Columbia University *(NY)*
Kweisi Mfume *(head of NAACP)*	Morgan State University *(MD)*
Walter Mondale *(former vice president)*	University of Minnesota
Toni Morrison *(writer)*	Howard University *(DC)*
Carol Mosely-Braun *(senator)*	Univ. of Illinois—Chicago
Al Neuharth *(founder, USA Today)*	University of South Dakota
Jessye Norman *(opera singer)*	University of Michigan
Antonia Novello *(former Surgeon General)*	University of Puerto Rico
Joyce Carol Oates *(writer)*	Syracuse University *(NY)*
Dan O'Brien *(decathlete)*	University of Idaho
Carroll O'Connor *(actor)*	University of Montana
Sandra Day O'Connor *(Supreme Court)*	Stanford University *(CA)*
Clarence Page *(newspaper columnist)*	Ohio University
Jane Pauley *(TV journalist)*	Indiana University
I. M. Pei *(architect)*	Mass. Institute of Technology

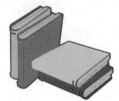

Theodor Geisl, better known as Dr. Seuss, author of The Cat in the Hat *and numerous other books, attended Dartmouth College. E.B. White, who wrote* Charlotte's Web, *went to Cornell University. And Judy Blume, author of books such as* Are You There God? It's Me, Margaret, *went to New York University.*

Who Went Where to College?

Graduate	College
Federico Peña *(secretary of transportation)*	University of Texas—Austin
Colin Powell *(military general, writer)*	City University of New York
Michael Quinlan *(head of McDonald's)*	Loyola University *(IL)*
Janet Reno *(attorney general)*	Cornell University *(NY)*
William Richardson *(congressman)*	Tufts University *(MA)*
Sally Ride *(astronaut)*	Stanford University *(CA)*
Cokie Roberts *(news analyst)*	Wellesley College *(MA)*
Fred Rogers *(Mister Rogers' Neighborhood)*	Rollins College *(FL)*
Roy Romer *(governor)*	Colorado State University
Maria Shriver *(journalist)*	Georgetown University *(DC)*
Jeff Smith *(TV chef, The Frugal Gourmet)*	Univ. of Puget Sound *(WA)*
Jimmy Smits *(actor)*	Cornell University *(NY)*
Olympia Snowe *(senator)*	University of Maine
Stephen Sondheim *(theater composer)*	Williams College *(MA)*
Steven Spielberg *(director, producer)*	Cal. State U.—Long Beach
Meryl Streep *(actress)*	Vassar College *(NY)*
Susan Stroman *(Broadway choreographer)*	University of Delaware
Amy Tan *(writer)*	San Jose State Univ. *(CA)*
Helen Thomas *(journalist)*	Wayne State University *(MI)*
Isaac Tigrett *(cofounder, Hard Rock Cafe)*	Centre College *(KY)*
Ted Turner *(media, CNN, TBS, TNT)*	Brown University *(RI)*
Anne Tyler *(writer)*	Duke University *(NC)*
Denzel Washington *(actor)*	Fordham University *(NY)*
Christine Todd Whitman *(governor)*	Wheaton College *(MA)*
Oprah Winfrey *(talk show host, producer)*	Tennessee State University
Alfre Woodard *(actress)*	Boston University *(MA)*

Colleges recognize the work of outstanding citizens by awarding them honorary degrees. For example, entertainer Bob Hope has received dozens of degrees in recognition not only of his comic and acting achievements, but also of his work on behalf of U. S. military personnel stationed around the world.

Race and ethnicity. The racial and ethnic mix of college students has changed considerably over the past several decades. The number of African-American and Hispanic students has grown, as has the number of Asian and Native American students.

The desegregation of the 1950s and 1960s was important in opening up many opportunities. Since then, colleges have worked hard to develop student bodies that better represent their communities. Many have designed programs that reach out to students of color. Some programs focus on promoting the college to increase applications. Others focus on providing services for students.

Over the past two decades, more than two dozen colleges that focus on the needs and concerns of Native Americans have been established throughout a dozen states in the west and midwest. Seven of these colleges, including Blackfeet Community College, Fort Peck Community College, and Little Big Horn College, are located in Montana.

In 1881, Tuskegee University was founded in Alabama to provide industrial training for black students. Famous American educator Booker T. Washington headed the school until 1915 and transformed it into an important industrial and agricultural center. The university has continued to expand its offerings into a variety of professional and liberal arts areas as well. In 1896, George Washington Carver moved to Tuskegee. While there, he conducted his famous experiments with peanuts and other crops. Important agricultural research continues at Tuskegee to this day.

Geography. The number of people who live in each state varies quite a lot across the country. In a similar way, the number of students who attend college in each state also varies.

By a wide margin, California has more college students than any other state. Each year about two million students attend college in California. Next on the list are New York, Texas, Florida, Illinois, and Michigan. At the other end are states like Alaska, Wyoming, Vermont, South Dakota, Montana, and North Dakota. Of course, these are also states that have relatively small populations.

When you decide to apply to college, you will be able to apply to schools in your own state as well as schools in other states. As it turns out, most students stay in their own state—over 80 percent. This is true in part because most states have large state university systems that charge you less if you are a resident. Therefore, you can go away to college without going too far from home. For many, this option is the best of both worlds!

While New York attracts a lot of college students, it actually loses more students to other states than it gains. In the fall of 1992, 21,609 freshmen came from out of state to New York. However, 24,826 left New York to be freshmen elsewhere.

Massachusetts, Pennsylvania, and New York bring in the most students from out of state. All three have many nationally known private colleges. In the fall of 1992, over 21,000 freshmen came to Massachusetts from out of state, while about 13,000 freshmen left for colleges in other states.

New Jersey's pattern is different. More students left New Jersey to go to college than came to New Jersey from other states. This is not surprising, though. Pennsylvania and New York have almost 300 four-year colleges between them. Thus, New Jersey students have many nearby choices.

How Many Students Are in Your State?

State	College Students in 1970	College Students in 1992
Alabama	103,936	230,537
Alaska	9,471	30,902
Arizona	109,619	275,999
Arkansas	52,039	97,435
California	1,257,245	1,977,248
Colorado	123,395	240,183
Connecticut	124,700	165,874
Delaware	25,260	42,763
Florida	235,525	618,285
Georgia	126,511	293,162
Hawaii	38,562	61,162
Idaho	34,567	57,798
Illinois	452,146	748,032
Indiana	192,666	298,912
Iowa	108,902	177,813
Kansas	102,485	169,418
Kentucky	98,591	188,320
Louisiana	120,728	204,379
Maine	34,134	57,977
Maryland	149,807	268,399
Massachusetts	303,808	422,976
Michigan	392,726	559,728
Minnesota	160,788	272,920
Mississippi	73,987	123,754
Missouri	183,930	296,617
Montana	30,062	39,844

In the fall of 1970, about 67,000 students were enrolled at U.S. colleges in American Samoa, Guam, Micronesia, the Northern Marianas, Palau, Puerto Rico, and the Virgin Islands. By the fall of 1992, the number of students had grown to more than 169,000.

How Many Students Are in Your State?

State	College Students in 1970	College Students in 1992
Nebraska	66,916	122,603
Nevada	13,669	63,877
New Hampshire	29,400	63,924
New Jersey	216,121	342,446
New Mexico	44,481	99,276
New York	806,479	1,059,772
North Carolina	171,925	383,453
North Dakota	31,495	40,470
Ohio	376,267	573,183
Oklahoma	110,156	182,105
Oregon	122,177	167,415
Pennsylvania	411,044	829,832
Rhode Island	45,896	79,165
South Carolina	69,518	171,443
South Dakota	30,639	37,596
Tennessee	135,103	242,970
Texas	442,225	938,526
Utah	81,687	133,083
Vermont	22,209	37,377
Virginia	151,915	354,172
Washington	183,544	276,484
West Virginia	63,153	90,252
Wisconsin	202,058	307,902
Wyoming	15,220	31,548
District of Columbia	77,158	81,909

The biggest increase in college enrollment over the past 25 years has come from states like Florida, Texas, and California. These states have rapidly growing populations. These states have also added many new colleges to their statewide systems.

Economic background. College was once a place for students from wealthy backgrounds. The land-grant colleges built in the latter half of the nineteenth century were intended to make college more available to students from all economic groups. Community colleges have also increased accessibility. They provide low-cost education with flexible schedules. The increase of federal assistance through school loan programs and grants also made college more accessible.

The government measures your socioeconomic background based on your parents' education, their occupations, and family income.

As recently as 1982, over 29 percent of students from the lowest socioeconomic background had *no* plans of attending college. By 1992, this group was only 8.1 percent. Even more dramatic: In 1982, about 38 percent of this same group planned to go to college directly after high school. But by 1992, over 80 percent planned to go to college directly after high school.

International students in the United States. Every year a large number of students come from other countries to study in the United States. In recent years, the number has grown. Now over 400,000 students come each year to the United States from other countries. (A large number of students from the United States go to study in other countries each year as well.)

The single largest group of foreign students who come each year is from South and East Asia. In 1992, more than 45,000 students came from China and more than 42,000 students from Japan. These students, along with those from India, Pakistan, Taiwan, Korea, and Malaysia, represent over half of all international students who come to the United States.

International Students in the United States

Country or Region of Origin	Number of Students in the United States in Fall 1992	Percentage of International Students in 1992
Brazil	4,540	1.0
Canada	20,970	4.8
China	45,130	10.3
Colombia	2,850	0.6
France	5,660	1.3
Germany	7,880	1.8
Greece	4,350	1.0
Hong Kong	14,020	3.2
India	35,950	8.2
Indonesia	10,920	2.5
Iran	4,090	0.9
Japan	42,840	9.8
Jordan	3,260	0.7
Korea	28,520	6.5
Lebanon	2,540	0.6
Malaysia	12,660	2.9
Mexico	7,580	1.7
Nigeria	2,490	0.6
Oceania*	4,300	1.0
Pakistan	8,020	1.8
Philippines	3,700	0.8
Saudi Arabia	3,750	0.9
Singapore	4,860	1.1
Spain	5,160	1.2
Taiwan	37,430	8.5
Thailand	8,630	2.0
Turkey	4,980	1.1
United Kingdom	7,830	1.7
Venezuela	3,440	0.8
Total**	438,620	100.0

*includes Australia and New Zealand   **includes other countries not listed

Where Did U.S. Presidents Attend College?

President	College
George Washington	did not attend
John Adams	Harvard College *(MA)*
Thomas Jefferson	College of William and Mary *(VA)*
James Madison	College of New Jersey (Princeton)
James Monroe	College of William and Mary *(VA)**
John Quincy Adams	Harvard College *(MA)*
Andrew Jackson	did not attend
Martin Van Buren	did not attend
William Henry Harrison	Hampden-Sydney College *(VA)*
John Tyler	College of William and Mary *(VA)**
James K. Polk	University of North Carolina
Zachary Taylor	did not attend
Millard Fillmore	did not attend
Franklin Pierce	Bowdoin College *(ME)*
James Buchanan	Dickinson College *(PA)*
Abraham Lincoln	did not attend
Andrew Johnson	did not attend
Ulysses S. Grant	U.S. Military Academy *(NY)*
Rutherford B. Hayes	Kenyon College *(OH)*
	Harvard Law School *(MA)*
James A. Garfield	Hiram College *(OH)**
	Williams College *(MA)*
Chester Alan Arthur	Union College *(NY)*
Grover Cleveland	did not attend
Benjamin Harrison	Miami University *(OH)*
William McKinley	Allegheny College *(PA)**

attended, but did not graduate

Before they were elected President of the United States, Woodrow Wilson served as president of Princeton University (NJ) and Dwight Eisenhower served as president of Columbia University (NY).

Where Did U.S. Presidents Attend College?

President	College
Theodore Roosevelt	Harvard University *(MA)*
William Howard Taft	Yale University *(CT)*
	Cincinnati Law School *(OH)*
Woodrow Wilson	Davidson College *(NC)**
	College of New Jersey
	University of Virginia Law School
Warren G. Harding	Ohio Central College
Calvin Coolidge	Amherst College *(MA)*
Herbert Hoover	Stanford University *(CA)*
Franklin D. Roosevelt	Harvard University *(MA)*
	Columbia Univ. Law School *(NY)*
Harry S. Truman	did not attend
Dwight D. Eisenhower	U.S. Military Academy *(NY)*
John F. Kennedy	Harvard University *(MA)*
Lyndon B. Johnson	SW Texas State Teachers Coll.
Richard M. Nixon	Whittier College *(CA)*
	Duke University Law School *(NC)*
Gerald Ford	University of Michigan
	Yale University Law School *(CT)*
Jimmy Carter	Georgia Southwestern College*
	Georgia Institute of Technology*
	United States Naval Aacademy *(MD)*
Ronald Reagan	Eureka College *(IL)*
George Bush	Yale University *(CT)*
Bill Clinton	Georgetown University *(DC)*
	Oxford University *(Britain)*
	Yale University Law School *(CT)*

*attended, but did not graduate

President Herbert Hoover was in the first freshman class at Stanford University, where he studied geology and mining. While at Stanford, he met his wife, Lou Henry, the only woman geology student then at Stanford.

Students with disabilities. The number of students with physical and learning disabilities has increased in recent years. Colleges are now more accessible than ever to students with special needs. Ramps, elevators, and other conveniences have been added. Academic and other special services for students have been added as well.

Technology has also made a difference. Medical advances and computers have combined to help people overcome many disabilities. Cultural changes have also made an important difference. Not too long ago, people with disabilities were often looked at in terms of what they could not do. Today, we tend to focus on what people can accomplish regardless of their disabilities.

First-generation students. Students whose parents and other ancestors did not attend college are often referred to as first-generation students. This term applies equally to those students who are immigrants to the United States and those whose families have been in the United States for 300 years. Many colleges have come to realize that some first-generation students have special needs when they first apply to college and start their first year. Some of these colleges have set up special programs that help make college more accessible to people who might not have thought they could or would ever attend college.

The bottom line. If you *want to go* to college, you *can go* to college. If you want college in your future, then it is there for you. And even though you may not get into your first choice, you will get into a college—one that offers you a good education and real opportunities.

4 WHERE ARE COLLEGES LOCATED?

Colleges are located everywhere! As the number of colleges in the United States has increased, so too has the variety of colleges.

Today, colleges and universities come in all sizes and settings. For example, you can find extremely large colleges in small towns and very small colleges in big cities.

You may not even need to leave home in order to get a college education. Instead, college can come to you: through the mail, through your television, and through your computer.

WHAT IS A CAMPUS?

If you hear that a college has a beautiful campus, you are hearing about the college's physical setting as well as its buildings. Sometimes these are referred to as buildings and grounds.

College campuses are located in a wide range of settings. Some colleges, like Temple University in Philadelphia and Wayne State University in Detroit, are located in the heart of a big city. These are examples of urban colleges.

Other colleges have rural campuses and might be set in ranch or farm country. Eastern Wyoming College in Torrington, Wyoming, and Castleton State College in Castleton, Vermont, are examples of rural colleges.

Many colleges, especially community colleges, have suburban campuses. Howard Community College in Maryland and Cuyahoga Community College in Ohio are examples of colleges located in the suburbs.

The Wolfson Campus (right), one of Miami-Dade Community College's five campuses, is located in the heart of downtown Miami and serves students in a highly populated urban area.

Still other colleges, like Clarkson University in New York and Williams College in Massachusetts, are located in the heart of small towns. The relationships between the towns and the colleges are extremely close.

College campuses vary in other ways. Some are hilly, others are flat. The buildings are spaced closely together on some campuses. On others, the buildings are spread apart with lots of space for walkways, fields, trees, or even ponds. The layout of the campus makes some colleges more accessible than others to students with physical disabilities or to students who commute.

The architecture also varies. For example, at many older colleges, you will see a lot of traditional red brick or stone buildings. Many colleges feature modern architecture. Some even have dramatic sculptures located around campus.

How you feel about a college's campus may be an important factor when you decide where to attend.

The Business Administration Building (right), like other buildings at the University of Texas at El Paso (UTEP), is designed in the style of buildings from the Himalayan kingdom of Bhutan. UTEP's campus provides the only example of this ancient architecture in the Western hemisphere.

WHAT ARE BRANCH CAMPUSES?

Sometimes a college is located in more than one place. The college may have a main or central campus. But then, in order to fill the needs of other students, the college sets up additional campuses in other locations. These campuses are often called branch campuses or extension centers. Branch campuses often open with temporary buildings. Permanent buildings are added later when student demand has grown.

For example, Shoreline Community College has its main campus just outside Seattle, Washington. In recent years, the communities to the east of Seattle have grown dramatically. In response, Shoreline Community College has opened the Northshore Center in Bothell, Washington. This center lets Shoreline bring college opportunities to more people in the community.

Sometimes branch campuses become equal in size or stature to the original campus. The college may become a multi-campus college. The campuses may or may not share a common administration. However, they often operate independently from each other.

Miami-Dade Community College in Florida began with one campus, the North Campus, that used temporary facilities for classrooms. In 1967, it opened a second campus, the Kendall Campus, which also began with temporary facilities. Today, the college has five major campuses. Several of the campuses now have their own extension centers.

OTHER TYPES OF CAMPUSES

You no longer need to go to a traditional college campus in order to study at the college level. A growing number of alternative opportunities are becoming available for taking college courses.

Distance learning centers allow students to take courses at other colleges without leaving their own campus. They also help colleges share resources.

Extended campuses. Most colleges provide opportunities for students to learn independently. For example, De Anza College, in Cupertino, California, has a Distance Learning Center. Students can complete most of their educational requirements through this center. Students can learn through interactive television. They can also take mixed-media courses that use combinations of videotapes, slides, audiotapes, workbooks, and computer software.

Correspondence studies. For various reasons, including physical disabilities, family responsibilities, or distance, not all students are able to go to a college campus to study. Correspondence studies provide opportunities for students to take courses through the mail. For instance, Western Kentucky University has over forty courses that students can take as correspondence courses.

Increasingly in years to come, students will be able to use the Internet to take college courses. The Internet is a large computer network that links computers all over the world.

Electronic courses. Computer technology has opened up another path to college. Now, if you have access to a computer and a modem, you may be able to take college courses on-line. Rogers State College in Claremore, Oklahoma, is a two-year college that offers such courses. You can complete graduation requirements at Rogers State College without having to go to any classes on campus. In coming years, many more colleges will offer courses through computer networks.

How Many Colleges Are in Your State?

State	Four-Year Colleges*	Two-Year Colleges*
Alabama	32	36
Alaska	6	6
Arizona	16	24
Arkansas	16	16
California	120	138
Colorado	28	24
Connecticut	28	17
Delaware	5	3
Florida	58	48
Georgia	49	32
Hawaii	6	8
Idaho	7	5
Illinois	81	64
Indiana	46	32
Iowa	38	27
Kansas	25	25
Kentucky	32	23
Louisiana	23	8
Maine	19	12
Maryland	32	23
Massachusetts	97	34
Michigan	61	35
Minnesota	36	31
Mississippi	19	19
Missouri	55	24
Montana	10	12

These numbers represent main campuses in fall 1994.

In addition to all of the colleges in the fifty states, there are over three dozen college campuses in Puerto Rico. Colleges are also located in American Samoa, Guam, the Northern Marianas, and the Virgin Islands.

How Many Colleges Are in Your State?

State	Four-Year Colleges*	Two-Year Colleges*
Nebraska	22	20
Nevada	4	4
New Hampshire	15	11
New Jersey	41	24
New Mexico	10	19
New York	173	92
North Carolina	53	64
North Dakota	10	10
Ohio	100	68
Oklahoma	23	20
Oregon	27	15
Pennsylvania	107	87
Rhode Island	10	2
South Carolina	32	24
South Dakota	16	7
Tennessee	45	23
Texas	87	79
Utah	7	8
Vermont	19	6
Virginia	41	38
Washington	27	34
West Virginia	21	10
Wisconsin	37	37
Wyoming	1	8
District of Columbia	13	0

These numbers represent main campuses in fall 1994.

Almost every state offers a full mix of colleges including four-year and two-year, public and private, large and small. Metropolitan areas like Philadelphia, Boston, New York, Chicago, and Los Angeles, offer dozens of choices.

The Largest Four-Year Colleges*

State	Largest College or University	Number*
Alabama	Auburn University	18,349
Alaska	University of Alaska—Anchorage	14,350
Arizona	Arizona State University	30,178
Arkansas	University of Arkansas—Fayetteville	11,508
California	University of California—Los Angeles	22,892
Colorado	University of Colorado—Boulder	20,006
Connecticut	University of Connecticut	12,059
Delaware	University of Delaware	14,932
Florida	University of Florida	27,473
Georgia	University of Georgia	22,301
Hawaii	University of Hawaii—Manoa	13,226
Idaho	Boise State University	12,997
Illinois	University of Illinois—Urbana	26,333
Indiana	Purdue University—West Lafayette	28,464
Iowa	Iowa State University	20,629
Kansas	University of Kansas	19,553
Kentucky	University of Louisville	21,864
Louisiana	Louisiana State University	20,040
Maine	University of Maine—Orono	9,161
Maryland	University of Maryland—College Park	23,331
Massachusetts	Northeastern University	21,381
Michigan	Michigan State University	30,760
Minnesota	University of Minnesota—Twin Cities	25,837
Mississippi	Mississippi State University	11,619
Missouri	Southwest Missouri State University	16,505
Montana	Montana State University	9,914

Based on total undergraduate students in fall 1993

In fall 1993, 14 different four-year colleges in California each had more than 15,000 undergraduate students. In 18 other states and the District of Columbia, no college campus had as many as 15,000 undergraduate students!!

The Largest Four-Year Colleges*

State	Largest College or University	Number*
Nebraska	University of Nebraska—Lincoln	19,829
Nevada	University of Nevada—Las Vegas	16,820
New Hampshire	University of New Hampshire	10,831
New Jersey	Kean College	10,233
New Mexico	University of New Mexico	20,004
New York	State University of New York—Buffalo	17,087
North Carolina	North Carolina State University	21,408
North Dakota	University of North Dakota	9,769
Ohio	Ohio State University	37,044
Oklahoma	University of Oklahoma	14,832
Oregon	University of Oregon	13,074
Pennsylvania	Penn State University—University Park	30,963
Rhode Island	University of Rhode Island	11,350
South Carolina	University of South Carolina	15,802
South Dakota	South Dakota State University	8,103
Tennessee	University of Tennessee—Knoxville	18,988
Texas	University of Texas—Austin	35,206
Utah	Brigham Young University	27,631
Vermont	University of Vermont	7,751
Virginia	Virginia Polytechnic Institute	19,115
Washington	University of Washington	24,938
West Virginia	West Virginia University	15,557
Wisconsin	Univeristy of Wisconsin—Madison	26,638
Wyoming	University of Wyoming	9,293
District of Columbia	University of the District of Columbia	9,985

*Based on total undergraduate students in fall 1993.

The main campus of Ohio State University in Columbus, Ohio, is the single largest campus in the United States. In fall 1993, over 37,000 undergraduate students and over 13,000 graduate students were enrolled.

EXCHANGE PROGRAMS AND CONSORTIUMS

Many colleges give you the opportunity to study at another college for up to a year. Your studies at the second college count toward your graduation requirements at the first. Two colleges may have an arrangement with each other for an exchange program: They exchange groups of students for one or more terms. The students get to broaden their experience at another type of campus, take courses that might not otherwise be available to them, and make new friends.

Sometimes when several colleges are located near each other they form a group called a consortium. Students at one college can take classes at the other colleges participating in the consortium. For example, Amherst College, Hampshire College, Mt. Holyoke College, University of Massachusetts, and Smith College are located within a few miles of each other. If you attend one of these colleges, you will be able to take certain courses at the other four colleges. You get some of the educational advantages of an exchange program without going away from your main college for a long period of time.

Pomona College in Claremont, California, and Colby College in Waterville, Maine, have an exchange program. A group of Pomona students spends half a school year studying at Colby while a group of Colby students studies at Pomona. In addition, Pomona College is one of the Claremont Colleges, a consortium that includes Claremont McKenna College, Harvey Mudd College, Pitzer College, Scripps College, and Claremont Graduate School.

COLLEGES OUTSIDE THE UNITED STATES

Increasingly, colleges are encouraging students to spend time studying at a college outside of the United States. No matter what your field of study, you can benefit from studying abroad.

Many foreign study programs are aimed at college juniors. These programs are referred to as junior year abroad. *Students may spend an entire year abroad, though many go for only half a year.*

If you are studying a foreign language, you will probably want to study in a country where that language is spoken. If you are studying business, economics, history, or government, then an international perspective would be of value to you. Even students who focus on American studies can benefit from learning how other countries view the United States.

Two-year and four-year colleges offer programs for international studies. The American Institute for Foreign Studies coordinates programs with many community colleges so that students can study outside the United States. Students at Santa Rosa Junior College in California, for example, can study in London, England. And students at Grambling State University in Louisiana have been able to study in countries such as Brazil, Mexico, China, India, Malaysia, and Kenya. If you attend Dartmouth College, you will have opportunities for foreign study in over two dozen countries throughout the world.

The American University in Paris and the American University in Cairo are two examples of American colleges based in other countries.

Students who want to spend all of their college years outside the United States can apply directly to a college based in another country. They can also apply to American colleges based in other countries. Choose wisely if you plan to study outside the United States. Be sure your studies will be recognized in the United States.

Colleges Around the World

Country/Province	College or University	Year Founded
Argentina	University of Buenos Aires	1821
Australia	University of Melbourne	1853
Brazil	Federal University	1920
China	Beijing University	1898
Costa Rica	University of Costa Rica	1843
Czech Republic	Charles University	1348
Egypt	Al-Azhar University	970
England	Merton College (Oxford)	1264
France	The Sorbonne	1257
Germany	University of Heidelberg	1386
India	University of Bombay	1857
Ireland	Trinity College	1592
Israel	Hebrew University—Jerusalem	1918
Italy	University of Bologna	1317
Japan	University of Tokyo	1877
Kenya	University of Nairobi	1956
Mexico	National Autonomous University of Mexico	1551
Morocco	al-Qarawiyin	859
The Netherlands	Leiden University	1575
Nigeria	University of Ibadan	1948
Ontario, Canada	University of Toronto	1827
Pakistan	University of the Punjab	1882
Philippines	University of the Philippines	1908
Poland	University of Krakow	1364
Portugal	University of Lisbon	1288
Quebec, Canada	McGill University	1821
Russia	St. Petersburg State University	1819
Scotland	University of St. Andrews	1411
South Africa	University of Cape Town	1829
Spain	The University of Salamanca	1218
Switzerland	University of Basel	1459
Taiwan	Soochow University	1900
Venezuela	Central University of Venezuela	1721

5

WHAT CAN I LEARN AT COLLEGE?

You can learn anything and everything! Even the smallest of colleges offer many areas of study and hundreds of different classes. Some classes provide broad overviews of a subject. Others focus on a very specific part of a subject.

Colleges have basic requirements that you must meet in order to graduate. In this chapter, you will learn about meeting them.

At college you also choose a subject of special interest. You then take classes that focus on that subject. In this chapter, we will give you an overview of many of these areas of study.

COLLEGE DEGREES

After you meet high school requirements, you graduate and receive a high school diploma.

Similarly, when you meet the requirements for the college you attend, you will receive a college diploma. You will also earn a degree, a title that the college grants you. The title indicates you have completed a specific program of study offered by a specific college.

What is a bachelor's degree? People earn a bachelor's degree when they complete graduation requirements for a four-year college. The two degrees that are granted most often in the United States are the B.A. (Bachelor of Arts) and the B.S. (Bachelor of Sciences).

A.B. also stands for Bachelor of Arts. Similarly, both B.Sc. and Sc.B. can also stand for Bachelor of Science.

Many smaller colleges offer only one degree, most often the B.A. In fact, graduating students may receive that title even if they have taken mostly science courses. Larger schools often offer both degrees. The student's area of study determines which degree is awarded at graduation.

Some schools offer other bachelor's degrees for students who have specialized in such areas as music, literature, education, or theology.

See page 68 for a list of other degrees.

What other kinds of degrees can I earn? Most two-year colleges do not grant bachelor's degrees. However, they do grant associate degrees, either Associate of Arts (A.A.) or Associate of Sciences (A.S.). Two-year colleges also award certificates. These indicate that a student has completed a smaller amount of work in a specific field.

When you hear that someone is a doctor, you might think automatically of a medical doctor. However, not all doctors are medical doctors. See the chart on the next page to see a list of other types of doctors.

Students with bachelor's degrees can continue their studies at an advanced level. You can earn a master's degree by completing an additional year or two of specialized studies. For example, if you study business administration at an advanced level, you may earn the title M.B.A., or Master in Business Administration. With an additional two to five years of very specialized and advanced study, you can earn a doctor's degree. The Ph.D., which stands for Doctor of Philosophy, is one of the more commonly earned doctorates.

What is an undergraduate? Students who have not yet earned their college degrees are called undergraduates. Once they have earned their bachelor's degrees and are enrolled in advanced studies, they are graduate students. As Chapter 1 noted, universities are usually made up of one or more undergraduate colleges as well as graduate schools offering advanced degrees.

Grades are usually the most important factor in determining who graduates with honors.

What is an honors graduate? Colleges honor their top students at graduation by awarding them a mark of distinction. You can graduate *cum laude*, with praise; *magna cum laude*, with great praise; or *summa cum laude*, with highest praise. These honors follow you throughout your life. They can help you continue your studies and get hired in your chosen field.

In the 1991-1992 school year, over one million students earned bachelor's degrees at U.S. colleges. During that same year, colleges awarded over 500,000 associate degrees, over 350,000 master's degrees, and over 40,000 doctor's degrees.

Different Kinds of College Degrees

Degree	Full Name of Degree
A.A.	Associate of Arts
A.A.S.	Associate of Applied Science
A.S.	Associate of Science
A.B. or B.A.	Bachelor of Arts
B.B.S.	Bachelor of Business Science
B.C.L.	Bachelor of Civil Law
B.D.	Bachelor of Divinity
B.F.A.	Bachelor of Fine Arts
B.Lit. or B.Litt	Bachelor of Literature
B.S. or B.Sc.	Bachelor of Science
Lit.B.	Bachelor of Literature
LL.B.	Bachelor of Laws
Mus.B.	Bachelor of Music
M.A.	Master of Arts
M.A.T.	Master of Arts in Teaching
M.B.A.	Master of Business Administration
M.C.E.	Master of Civil Engineering
M.F.A.	Master of Fine Arts
M.P.A.	Master of Public Administration
M.S.	Master of Science
M.S.W.	Master of Social Work
D.B.A.	Doctor of Business Administration
D.D.	Doctor of Divinity
D.D.S.	Doctor of Dental Surgery
D.S. or D.Sc.	Doctor of Science
D.V.M.	Doctor of Veterinary Medicine
Ed.D	Doctor of Education
J.D.	Doctor of Jurisprudence (Doctor of Law)
L.L.D.	Doctor of Laws
M.D.	Doctor of Medicine
Ph.D.	Doctor of Philosophy

COURSES AND CREDITS

Right now you probably study anywhere from five to seven subjects during the school year. Think of each subject as a course. As you enter high school, you have more flexibility about which courses you take. For example, you may still have to study science in high school. However, you may be able to choose which science courses you take.

College courses are similar to courses you already take. They're taught at a higher level, but you'll be ready to study at that level when you get to college. Full-time college students take three to six courses at a time. Courses generally meet three times each week for fifty minutes or twice each week for an hour and fifteen minutes at a time. Some classes meet only once a week, but for a three-hour session. Many science classes have an additional session each week in which students gain practical experience in a laboratory.

Some science courses require students to meet more than once each week in a lab.

For each course that you take, you earn credits. Think of college credits as time. Most colleges assign one credit for each hour that the course meets during the week. You earn three credits for most courses and four credits for many science courses. However, some colleges assign one credit or unit for each course you take.

While most courses offer three or four credits, some offer fewer or more. For example, some review courses might only run for a few weeks and only offer one or two credits. Other classes, especially in math and foreign languages, meet four or five times a week.

At colleges that assign one credit per hour you are in class each week, you will need about 120 credits altogether to graduate. This equals 40 classes with three credits each—and fewer classes if you take courses offering more credits. The actual number depends on the college you attend and the specific program you study.

WHAT ARE DISTRIBUTION REQUIREMENTS?

These required courses are sometimes called core curriculum, foundation courses, or general education requirements.

As part of their graduation requirements, colleges often require you to take courses in a variety of different fields. While you might be allowed to choose the specific courses you take to meet these requirements, you must choose them from the categories selected by the college. Because these courses are distributed over several subject areas, they are often called distribution requirements.

Colleges also have other general requirements for their graduates, such as English, math, and cultural diversity requirements.

Colleges divide subjects into different groups such as natural sciences, social sciences, and humanities. These divisions are described later in this chapter. To fulfill distribution requirements, you must often take a certain number of courses in each of these areas.

Sample Distribution Requirements

Distribution Requirements for Bachelor of Arts Degree at Ohio Wesleyan University

Social Sciences. Three courses selected from subject areas such as black world studies, history, politics and government, geography, economics, journalism, psychology, and sociology/anthropology.

Natural Sciences. Three courses selected from subject areas such as botany and microbiology, chemistry, physics, geology, astronomy, and zoology.

Humanities. Three courses selected from subject areas such as English, French, German, Spanish, humanities and classics, philosophy, religion, theatre and dance, black world studies, and women's studies.

Arts. One course selected from subject areas such as music, theatre, dance, fine arts, and English.

College Majors, Minors, and Electives

While you are at college, you choose an area of study in which you will concentrate most of your time. This area is called your major.

How do I choose a major? During your freshman or sophomore year, you will meet with your advisor—a teacher or counselor who is assigned to help you choose a major. Your advisor helps you complete paperwork and other requirements for declaring the major. At larger universities, you must often apply during your freshmen year to be accepted into a specific program of study.

Some majors help you prepare for graduate studies. For instance, pre-medical (or pre-med) majors help prepare you for medical school and pre-law majors help prepare you for law school.

How do I complete a major? Departments are groups of professors who teach the same subject area. Each department sets up requirements for a major field of study. For instance, to major in English, you might need to take a minimum of ten English courses. The department may require you to take at least one course on world literature and one course on Shakespeare. You may also be required to take a group of related courses. For instance, you might take three or more courses on American literature or on the novel.

Requirements for English majors vary from college to college. Requirements for others majors also vary. Sometimes you have a lot of choice about the courses you take. But in other cases, the department tells you what to take.

Your faculty advisor or the Dean's office can help you complete any paperwork needed for changing your major.

What if I change my mind? Many students find they would like to switch to another major. You are allowed to change your mind as long as you complete the requirements for the new major.

At the University of North Carolina at Chapel Hill, students are first admitted to the General College. As freshmen and sophomores, they concentrate on completing their general education requirements. During the last half of their sophomore year, they are accepted into an upper level college at which they complete their major requirements. These colleges include a college of arts and sciences, a school of education, a school of pharmacy, and the Kenan-Flagler business school.

*Students can gradu-
ate with a double
major by completing
requirements for two
majors. Students who
want to teach high
school often double
major in education
and in the field they
want to teach.*

What is a minor? Your major is your area of specialization. You may also want to concentrate in a second area because it interests you or because it helps you in your major field of study. However, you many not want to complete all the major requirements in this field.

Many colleges provide opportunities to minor in subjects. You still need to complete certain requirements, but they are fewer, for instance, six courses instead of ten. Suppose you decide to major in Spanish. You may also be interested in Hispanic drama. In that case, you may choose to major in Spanish and minor in theater.

*Some electives are
specific. You might be
required to take a
history course, for
instance, but you can
pick which one.
Other electives are
general—you can
choose any course
you want.*

What are electives? So far, we have looked at general and major requirements. In addition to required courses, you will be able to take other courses of your choosing. Courses you elect to take—which you are not required to take—are called electives. They provide opportunities to take additional courses in your major, courses taught by a particularly noted professor, or courses just for fun. Students can use electives as well for their minor or for a second major.

Divisions, Disciplines, and Departments

Colleges combine subject areas into groups called divisions. At larger universities, these divisions might actually be entire colleges or schools, such as a college of arts and sciences or a school of journalism.

Each subject area is a discipline. The people who teach in that discipline make up a department. Sometimes a department will cover more than one discipline. For example, the disciplines of French, Spanish, and other languages may make up the modern languages department.

Some subjects are interdisciplinary because they combine disciplines. For example, human development often combines biology and psychology to look at the nature of humans.

The way departments are combined varies. One college may have a *modern* languages department, which includes only currently spoken languages. The professors who teach Latin and Greek might be in a separate department, such as Classics. At another college, the Latin and Greek professors may be combined with the French and Spanish professors in a *foreign* languages department.

The way divisions are organized also varies. The business administration program at some colleges is so large that it is its own division made up of management, marketing, accounting, finance, human resources, and production disciplines. Elsewhere, the program may be so small that it is a single discipline within social sciences. Mathematics may be grouped with natural sciences, engineering, computer science, or humanities.

When you look at colleges, look at how departments are organized. Be sure the college offers the specific area in which you are interested.

NATURAL AND PHYSICAL SCIENCES

Many disciplines focus on the way the natural or physical world works. They are grouped together in natural science or physical science divisions. Many science courses require you to spend time in a lab conducting hands-on experiments. Math skills are very important. You often have to memorize new vocabulary, much of it unfamiliar.

Biology. Biology is the study of human, animal, and plant life. Fields within biology are disciplines in their own right at many larger colleges. For example, *botany* focuses on plant life while *zoology* focuses on animal life. The smallest units of life—molecules and cells—are not considered to be either animal or plant. *Molecular biology* and *cellular biology* focus on these building blocks of life.

Other important branches of biology study entire organisms, looking at their structure (*anatomy*), growth and development (*developmental biology*), and function (*physiology*). The field of *population biology* combines two fields: *ecology* (the study of populations in their environment) and *genetics* (the study of heredity).

Chemistry. Chemistry is the study of substances that make up the natural world and how adding or removing energy from these substances changes them. *Analytical chemistry* looks at what makes up substances. *Inorganic chemistry* focuses on the properties and reactions of all chemical elements except for those containing carbon and hydrogen. Carbon compounds (those containing carbon) are the focus of *organic chemistry*.

Physics. Perhaps the broadest field in the natural sciences, physics looks at how all the parts of the universe interact. *Classical physics* focuses on physical forces such as gravity, electricity, and magnetism. *Modern physics* moves beyond the traditional theories and looks at the atomic world, semiconductors, and modern communications. Major fields within physics include *mechanics*, the study of objects in motion; *thermodynamics*, the study of heat and energy transformation; and *optics*, the study of light.

Earth sciences. Several important fields make up the earth sciences. The most prominent field is probably *geology*, the study of the planet earth. *Physical geology* looks at the composition of the planet, while *historical geology* looks at the earth's evolution (how the earth has changed over millions of years). Other fields include *paleontology*, the study of prehistoric life; *petrology*, the study of rocks; and *mineralogy*, the study of minerals. Other earth sciences include *meteorology*, the study of the earth's atmosphere and weather, and *oceanography*, the study of the oceans.

Astronomy. Astronomy studies the bodies of the universe, such as planets, meteors, comets, and stars. Within astronomy are branches that track the positions of these bodies and that study their chemical composition and physical forces. An important branch of astronomy is *cosmology*, which looks at the universe as a whole.

Combined sciences. Many fields combine two branches of science. For example, *geophysics* studies the effect of physical forces on the earth (e.g., earthquakes). *Biochemistry* studies the chemical composition of living organisms.

SOCIAL AND BEHAVIORAL SCIENCES

The way the physical world works is central to the natural sciences. The way the human world works is central to the social sciences. The social sciences look at individuals and society: human behavior and the interaction people have with each other and with the institutions set up to organize our lives.

Psychology. The behavior of individuals is the main focus of psychology. Animal behavior is also important. *Child* and *developmental psychology* look at how experiences and age affect behavior. *Abnormal psychology* emphasizes behavior that is not in the mainstream of expected and accepted behavior. *Experimental psychology* uses lab and other research to learn more about patterns of behavior. *Industrial psychology* explores behavior in the workplace. *Educational psychology* looks at how people learn and ways to help people make educational and career decisions. Counseling and therapy—helping people with problems—are at the heart of *clinical psychology*.

Sociology. Sociology emphasizes the group and society. It looks at group behavior and the role of institutions such as marriage, the family, religion, schools, the legal system, and organizations. Roles that people are expected to play, based on factors such as class, religion, profession, gender, and age, are also studied. *Demography* is the study of population. Other areas include *criminology,* the study of legal systems and crime; *deviance*, which looks at behaviors that violate society's expectations; *urban sociology*, which focuses on behavior in cities; and *gerontology*, which focuses on the roles and behaviors of the elderly.

Social psychology. This important field, which draws on both sociology and psychology, looks at the relationship between individuals and groups. Psychologists examine how behavior is affected by groups and institutions. Sociologists focus on small group behavior and the ways groups and institutions affect individuals.

Anthropology. Anthropology looks at the physical and cultural development of humans. It also draws on natural sciences and history. *Physical anthropology*, which draws on biology, studies the evolution of humans and how they adapt to their environment over time. *Cultural anthropology* studies the development of societies, language, and culture.

Political science. Political science is the study of government. *Comparative government* looks at governments around the world. *Political theory* examines the ways in which governments such as democracies, dictatorships, and constitutional monarchies, are organized. *Politics* looks at how things get done: how elections are conducted and how bills become laws. *Public administration* is the study of how people govern, write budgets, and put policy into action. *Institutions* such as the presidency, Congress, the judicial system, lobbyists, and the media are also studied.

Economics. Economics studies systems of money and how goods and services are produced, distributed, and consumed. *Microeconomics* looks at the supply and demand of goods and services. *Macroeconomics* focuses on broad issues such as employment and national income. *Money and banking* focuses on how money is created and how the banking system is structured and operates.

ARTS AND HUMANITIES

The ways in which humans think about themselves and their place in the world make up the humanities. The ways in which humans use their imagination to express themselves creatively make up the arts.

History. Most colleges place history with either social sciences or humanities. History is the study of all that has taken place in the past. Special emphasis is given to activities of individuals and societies. You can specialize by studying certain regions, for instance Asian or African history. You can also specialize by studying time periods, for example, nineteenth-century history throughout the world. You can specialize in other ways too, studying the history of war, women, industrialization, and so forth.

Philosophy. Philosophy is the study of the basic principles of our lives and the world around us. Major branches include *metaphysics*, which tries to define reality; *epistemology*, the study of knowledge; *aesthetics*, the study of how we define what is beautiful; and *ethics*, the study of how we make moral judgments. *Logic* is an important branch that looks at how we can build arguments that reach valid conclusions.

Religion. Religion looks at people's views about God and the universe and how their beliefs shape their way of life. Most colleges offer studies of Jewish and Christian traditions. Other religions are also taught to give students a well-rounded view. Comparative religion looks for similarities and differences among religions. Ethics courses study contemporary issues that are much debated in society.

Classics. Most programs in the classics focus on the study of ancient Greece and Rome as well as other ancient cultures. You are often expected to learn either Latin or Greek. You might study not only the history and culture of great civilizations, but also the outstanding works of literature that these civilizations produced.

English. Students who major in English usually focus on either *writing* or *literature*. Those who specialize in writing may take many courses on the art of constructing novels, short stories, plays, and poems. Those who specialize in literature learn to analyze plots, themes, characters, and style. Most literature courses focus on works that were written in English. World literature courses introduce students to the works of great authors regardless of the language in which they wrote.

Performing arts. Many courses in drama and cinema are similar to literature courses: You read or view the great works of others. Other courses focus on performance. These courses train actors, directors, sound and lighting technicians, stage-hands, and other behind-the-scenes workers.

Courses in music, art, and dance can be history or studio courses. In history classes, you might take survey courses that give you broad overviews of the works of others. You might also take courses that narrow the focus. For example, you might study Italian opera, French Impressionist painting, or Russian ballet.

Studio courses give you direct experience. You might spend time in a studio singing, practicing an instrument, composing music, sculpting, painting, or choreographing a new dance.

ENGINEERING

How scientific and mathematical theories are applied to meet the challenges of our everyday world is central to engineering. There are over 25 major specialities within engineering. Many of these have their own subdivisions. Several major ones are described below.

Chemical engineering. Chemical engineering students learn to develop the processes and equipment that are used to make new materials and products. The transformation of petroleum (oil) into plastics and other materials, the development of synthetic rubber, and the process of removing salt from ocean water (desalination) all fall within the field of chemical engineering.

Civil engineering. Civil engineering focuses on structure—buildings, foundations, construction, road paving, and so forth. Civil engineering also deals with infrastructure—the design of networks of roads, bridges, and tunnels, and planning how reservoirs, dams, water lines, and sewer lines work together to serve a community. Major fields within civil engineering include *construction*, *surveying*, *soils*, *urban planning*, and *transportation*.

Electrical engineering. The field of electrical engineering focuses on the use of electric power and signals. It touches on telecommunications, computers, medical technology, and broadcast media. Major branches include *electric power and machinery*, generating and distributing electric power; *electronics*, transmitting and processing information by circuits and devices; *communications and control*, using information to perform tasks; and *computer engineering* (see page 86).

Mechanical engineering. Machines are at the heart of mechanical engineering. Some mechanical engineers specialize in *machines* themselves, their design and operation, and the materials used to build them. Others might specialize in either *fluid* or *thermal* (heat) *sciences*. *Robotics*, the use of machinery to perform human tasks, is a fast-growing field within mechanical engineering. It also has strong ties to electrical engineering.

Industrial engineering. Closely tied to fields within business administration (production and operations), industrial engineering looks at the management of industrial production. Cost, safety, budgeting, quality control, and planning for the efficient use of machines and human resources are all concerns of industrial engineering.

Other fields. *Aeronautical engineering* focuses on the development of aircraft for both civilian and military use. *Aerospace engineering*, which is concerned with vehicles flown outside the earth's atmosphere, is closely related. Often part of civil engineering, *environmental engineering* is concerned with matters such as water supply, air pollution, and disposal of solid and hazardous wastes. *Materials science* engineers specialize in the use of resources such as metals, ceramics, and plastics to create products. Their expertise is very important to engineers in other fields. *Military engineering* applies the tools of engineering to military purposes. *Mining engineers* study ways of finding and extracting mineral deposits.

Nuclear engineers work on developing and using nuclear energy for power and other purposes. *Safety engineers* work in all the engineering fields developing ways to prevent accidents and improve job and public safety.

MATHEMATICS AND COMPUTER SCIENCE

Mathematics departments can be found within science, humanities, or engineering divisions. They are also often linked with computer science departments. A higher percentage of students take math courses than any other type of course, with the possible exception of English. The field of computer science is rapidly expanding. As with math, computer science skills are important tools for success in other fields of study.

Mathematics. Most students are required to take math courses in college. For many, the tools learned in algebra, geometry, trigonometry, and calculus form an important foundation for work in other fields. Logic skills developed in math are important in all fields, including humanities. Math majors may focus on *applied math* (using math to solve practical problems) or *pure math* (studying the theories of math).

Computer science. Today, computer skills are as important as basic communication and math skills. Students who major in computer science often choose between the *hardware* and *software* sides of computers. The hardware side, which can be taught through *computer engineering*, focuses on the machinery itself, the design of computers and systems, and the manufacture of components. The software side emphasizes *languages* that run computers. You can learn existing languages or applications such as networking. And you may learn to create your own programs. Computer courses are also taught outside computer science departments. For example, courses that teach you how to use computers to manage information are often found in business administration programs.

FOREIGN LANGUAGES

At many colleges, students must study a foreign language in order to graduate. Each college sets up its own requirements. If you study a foreign language in high school, you may be able to meet the requirement before entering college.

Many colleges group French, Spanish, Italian, and Portuguese together in a Romance Languages department. These languages are called Romance languages because they developed from the Latin spoken in late Roman times.

Knowing another language can be helpful to you in many careers. Business students can improve their job opportunities with international firms if they speak a second language. Knowing a second language will be helpful to you if you have an interest in research, whether in history, music, archaeology, psychology, or any other field. For instance, if your field is music, then German and Italian are especially important.

Spending your junior year abroad provides a great opportunity to master another language.

While Spanish and French are the most commonly taught languages, today you can learn almost any language you want. Brigham Young University (BYU) in Provo, Utah, offers a particularly wide range of languages. Some are listed below.

Languages Taught at BYU

Afrikaans	German	Polish
American Sign	Hebrew	Portuguese
Arabic	Hindi	Russian
Bulgarian	Hungarian	Spanish
Cantonese	Icelandic	Swahili
Czech	Italian	Swedish
Danish	Japanese	Thai
Dutch	Korean	Ukranian
Finnish	Mandarin	Vietnamese
French	Norwegian	Welsh

OTHER PROGRAMS

In addition to the areas of study already described, you can choose from many others, depending on the college you attend.

Agriculture and forestry. Students can specialize in several areas. *Agricultural business* focuses on how to manage a farm or a ranch. *Agronomy* emphasizes crop production and *animal science* emphasizes breeding and raising farm animals and livestock. *Horticulture* focuses on ornamental plants, fruits, and vegetables; landscaping design is a related program. Students might also study *range science* or *water management*. Students who are thinking of becoming *veterinarians* may take agricultural courses as well.

Students in *forestry* learn to manage forests for environmental and recreational purposes. They also can study how to harvest timber, maple syrup, and other forest products; land surveying; and the use of trees and other plants in urban settings.

Business administration. Areas of study include *management*, coordinating a company's resources; *human resource management,* managing the people in a company; *production*, coordinating how goods and services are produced; *marketing*, overseeing goods and services brought to the marketplace; *accounting*, managing the financial information; *finance*, making sure a company has the resources it needs; *organizational behavior,* developing the company's structure so that people can work effectively; *business law*, understanding laws relevant to how business is conducted; and *management information systems* (MIS), managing a company's data, mostly by computer.

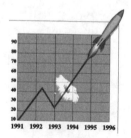

Medical and health sciences. If you are thinking about being a doctor, dentist, optometrist, or veterinarian, then you will want to take a program that will prepare you for graduate school. Check with colleges in which you are interested about the specific course of study they recommend. Premed students often major in biology.

Many colleges offer either two-year or four-year nursing programs that help prepare students to meet state requirements. Since not all colleges have programs in career areas such as pharmacy, physical therapy, or nutrition, you will want to look carefully for these programs. Many two-year colleges provide training as emergency medical technicians (EMT), radiology technicians, and physician's assistants.

Education. In order to be a teacher, you need to be certified by the state in which you will teach. Requirements for elementary and pre-school teachers are more strict than those for middle and high school teachers. Not all colleges have programs that meet state standards for elementary and pre-school teachers. More have programs for middle and high school teachers. You will want to check on a college-by-college basis.

Military programs. You can combine college with a military career by attending colleges run by branches of the military such as the United States Air Force. Or you may enroll in a Reserved Officers Training Corps (ROTC) program. Many colleges throughout the country offer ROTC. One benefit of participating in a military program, whether through a military academy or ROTC, is that you will usually receive help paying for some or all of your college costs.

OTHER REQUIREMENTS

As we have seen, you must meet certain requirements to earn your college degree. You must take a number of courses and earn a certain number of credits. You may also have to show a certain level of ability in English, math, and foreign language. You also declare a major and meet the specific requirements for that major. Some colleges will have additional requirements, such as keeping your grades at or above a certain level. As we've noted before, check what the requirements are for each individual college.

Information about requirements can be found in college catalogs (Chapter 7) or by talking with your faculty advisor (Chapter 12).

 ## ANYTHING AND EVERYTHING!

We started this chapter by noting that you can learn anything and everything at college. You've now read about a wide range of disciplines that you can study. In the next chapter, you'll also learn about internships and independent studies. These provide you with an opportunity to build your own course around something of special interest to you.

Some colleges let you design an independent major. You work closely with your advisor to put together an entire program of study—not just one course—of special interest to you. If you have a clear idea of what you want to study, then find a college that offers that program or find one that will let you build your own.

Many colleges will let individual students design an independent major. At Hampshire College in Massachusetts, all students design their own programs of study. In addition, the college requires all students to perform community service.

6 HOW WILL I LEARN AT COLLEGE?

You will learn in all sorts of ways! Chapter 5 describes the many different subjects you can choose when you attend college. But it is not only the subjects you study that vary. In this chapter, we will look at the different ways you can learn—in the classroom and out.

We'll start by looking at how colleges set up their school year. We'll take a look at the different ways you can attend class. We will then look at the tools you can use to study—the library, books, computers, and multimedia tools among them. You'll find that college is much more than just sitting in a classroom and listening to a professor talk!

THE COLLEGE CALENDAR

Colleges do not all use the same school year. They have different starting and ending dates. They also have different ways to divide the school year.

Many colleges offer optional summer terms. Some students attend a different college during the summer—they take classes that might not be available to them otherwise.

What is a semester? Many college school years are divided into two terms called semesters. Most semesters last 16 to18 weeks. Fall semesters start in August or September and end in December or January. Spring semesters start in January or February and end in late April or May. Most students take four or five classes each semester.

Some colleges have a 4-1-4 or a 4-4-1 calendar. Students attend two terms, each term lasting four months. Students also have one month of special studies, either between terms (4-1-4) or at the end of the year (4-4-1). Rollins College in Winter Park, Florida, has a 4-1-4 calendar. Transylvania University in Lexington, Kentucky, has a 4-4-1 calendar.

Are there other types of college calendars? Some colleges have three trimesters. Each lasts about 15 weeks. Most full-time students take classes two trimesters per year. (Attending all three can shorten the time needed to graduate.) Since trimesters are shorter than semesters, the pace of each course is quicker. You cover the same amount of material, but in a shorter time span.

Colleges that use the quarter term system divide the year into four terms. Each lasts about 11 weeks. Most full-time students attend three terms per year, usually in the fall, winter, and spring. In a quarter term, you take fewer courses at a time. Course are taught at a faster pace and meet more hours each week than semester courses do.

At Colorado College in Colorado, Cornell College in Iowa, and Tusculum College in Tennessee, students take only one course at a time. Each course lasts about three and a half weeks, with a few days off between courses. Students take eight or nine courses each year.

Two Different College Calenders

Semester Calendar The University of New Mexico 1996-1997	Quarter Calendar Northwestern University 1996-1997

1996 Fall Semester

August 26	Instruction begins
September 7	Last day to add or change classes
October 5	Last day to drop class without grade
November 16	Last day to withdraw without Dean's approval
December 14	Instruction ends
December 14-21	Final examinations
December 21	Semester ends

1997 Spring Semester

January 21	Instruction begins
February 1	Last day to add or change classes
March 1	Last day to drop class without grade
April 12	Last day to withdraw without Dean's approval
May 10	Instruction ends
May 10-17	Final examinations
May 17	Semester ends

1996 Fall Quarter

September 24	Classes begin
September 30	Last day to add or change classes
November 1	Last day to drop class
November 1	Last day to withdraw without academic review
December 7	Classes end
December 9-14	Final examinations
December 14	Quarter ends

1997 Winter Quarter

January 6	Classes begin
January 13	Last day to add or change classes
February 14	Last day to drop class
February 14	Last day to withdraw without academic review
March 15	Classes end
March 17-22	Final examinations
March 22	Quarter ends

1997 Spring Quarter

April 1	Classes begin
April 8	Last day to add or change classes
May 9	Last day to drop class
May 9	Last day to withdraw without academic review
June 7	Classes end
June 9-14	Final examinations
June 14	Quarter ends

Are All Classrooms the Same?

College courses can be taught in different settings based on the number of students, the professor's teaching style, the subject, and other factors.

Some professors give very clear personal opinions. Others offer many points of view. Expect to be challenged about your ideas and opinions— that's part of the excitement of college!

Lectures. In many courses, professors stand in front of students and talk—or lecture—about the topic being covered. They might use slides, films, videos, recordings, computers, and handouts with additional information. Some may provide time during their lecture for students to ask questions. And others may even ask questions for students to answer during their lectures.

Lectures can be given in regular classrooms, much like the ones used in middle and high school. The classes often have between 15 and 40 students. However, you may find yourself in a big lecture hall or auditorium that holds hundreds of students. In these larger lecture classes, students are often divided into smaller discussion groups that meet with teaching assistants once a week.

During lectures, students usually take lots of notes for later review. Some bring tape recorders so that they can listen to the class later. Large lecture classes may be videotaped; you can then review the videotapes at a later date.

A history professor may lecture about the American Civil War from a Union perspective, then ask you to read from the Confederate perspective. You would then learn both points of view about the war.

Expect to have a reading assignment that you should complete before class. Lectures may cover the same ground in more detail or summarize what you have read. Sometimes you may read material that differs from the point of view your professor presents in class. This contrast provides you with a wider range of views.

Discussion classes. Not all classes are lectures. Some classes combine lectures with classroom discussions or even emphasize discussion. These classes are usually smaller so that all students can participate fully.

Discussion classes have several formats. Sometimes professors begin with a brief lecture and then invite your reaction and discussion. Others often begin with discussion, asking questions that help guide the students toward making discoveries on their own.

For example, in a political science class, you may look at how television influences who gets elected to public office. The professor might ask you to summarize the assigned reading about the topic. Other students add their own views about the pros and cons of television and how much of a role it really does have. The professor steers the discussion, making sure all sides are covered and that certain key points are raised.

In a seminar, you often sit in a circle or around large tables. You might even meet in a lounge or at a professor's home. The informal setting helps encourage everyone to participate.

What are seminars? In many ways, seminars are similar to discussion classes. However, they are usually taken by juniors and seniors majoring in the same field. Class size is small, often fewer than 15 students, so that everyone can participate fully. In fact, you are expected to participate!

Seminars usually focus on narrower topics. For example, instead of a course on "The American Novel," a seminar may focus on the novels of Mark Twain. Seminars often meet once a week for three hours. Discussions can then be detailed. Students learn from each other, challenging or supporting each other's views and defending their own.

Some labs may be scheduled. You attend on a specific day at a specific time. Other labs are open. You spend a certain amount of time each week at your convenience or you spend as much time as is needed to complete your work.

What happens in a lab class? Laboratories are for hands-on experience. You go to your regular lectures and then spend time in a lab. You often earn more credits for a course with a lab than you earn in other courses.

Natural science courses frequently include labs. You might study cells under a microscope in a biology lab, find the amount of acid in a solution in a chemistry lab, or study the effects of gravity on a falling object in a physics lab.

Math, computer, and foreign language courses may also have labs. But their main purpose is to give students an opportunity to practice what has been taught.

Courses in the social sciences, engineering, and many other fields may also use labs. For example, in a psychology lab you might learn how to train an animal to behave in a particular way.

How do field studies differ from labs? Labs are controlled settings. While you might not know what the results of your research will be, you are in control of all the factors: temperature, lighting, time, and so forth. Field studies take you away from a controlled setting and into the real world. Instead of studying a leaf under a microscope, you might observe the growth of plants in the woods. You might look at different layers of soils near an earthquake fault line or study people's behavior when a traffic light turns yellow.

Labs and field studies give you the chance to apply the theories you learn in the classroom.

Both labs and field studies emphasize how you conduct research and experiments. You are trained to use equipment and to determine the purpose of your research. You are taught how to gather your observations and then how to record them in a way that will let you reach logical conclusions. Learning *how* to do good research is as important as doing the research itself.

Are there opportunities to study on my own?

In addition to the classes that you take with other students, many colleges offer opportunities for you to study independently. In fact, many colleges will strongly encourage you to take at least one course of independent study, especially during your junior or senior year.

Independent study. Would you like to study something in-depth that really interests you, even if it is not available as a regular college course? Independent studies provide you with that chance.

In an independent study you work one-on-one with a professor who agrees to sponsor your work. You set goals with the professor and then develop plans for achieving your goals. Your plans include how you will study and how often you will meet.

The possibilities of what you can do are endless! You can research how pollution is affecting a nearby pond, study a disease that has affected your family, write a full-length play, build a machine, or even start a company!

Not all college courses are offered on a regular basis. Some are offered only occasionally, perhaps only once every two years. (The college catalog will have this information.) Independent study gives you the chance to study the material taught in these courses, but at a time that fits your own schedule.

Studios and practice rooms. For many courses in the arts, you work in studios and practice rooms to develop your skills and techniques. Art students draw, paint, and sculpt in studios. You often work on your own, but may meet in groups, especially when working with a model. Performing arts majors spend hours alone vocalizing, practicing an instrument, learning dance steps, or even stretching muscles. You spend still more hours rehearsing with others in choirs, small ensembles, bands, orchestras, plays, and dance troupes.

Self-paced learning. Some classes are set up to allow you to work at your own pace. In many self-paced classes, you go to a learning lab to get your reading and homework assignments. You may be able to study in the lab itself, using computers or other equipment. You can also check out special materials, including books and videotapes. Tests are often administered by someone who works in the lab—an instructor or an aide. As long as you successfully complete all requirements within a set amount of time, you complete the course.

Self-paced learning is especially helpful for many remedial, developmental, and preparatory courses. These are courses that help you strengthen your skills and bring them up to the college level. For example, many students need to catch up with their math skills to the level needed for other classes. Self-paced learning is also seen in areas such as office technology.

Sometimes students cannot attend regular classes or work at a consistent pace during the year. Self-paced classes are helpful to these students.

Self-paced classes enable some students to finish a class early and move on to the next level. They also help students who need a longer period of time to complete the course.

Can I combine work with my studies? Many colleges have special programs that allow you to combine your education with work. The reasons for combining the two vary. Sometimes having the chance to earn money to pay for college is the main reason. Even in those cases, though, the chance to apply what you've learned in class to a setting in the real world is very important.

Cooperative education is sometimes called work-study or work-based learning. As we will see in Chapter 11, the term work-study *also refers to programs that help students pay for college by working on campus in paid jobs.*

Cooperative education. Students who want to combine their studies with jobs that help them pay for their education can participate in cooperative education (or co-op) programs. Students have the opportunity to gain practical experience working in their chosen field.

Many co-op students alternate between college and work. They may spend one term at college, followed by a term at a co-op job, followed by college again. At some colleges, they can repeat this pattern. In some cases, students combine work with studies. They take fewer classes at a given time and increase their work schedule.

Some colleges will allow students to apply co-op work experience toward meeting their graduation requirements. Even when co-op work does not count toward graduation requirements, you can earn money while gaining very valuable career experience.

Some students who participate in cooperative education at Maui Community College in Hawaii gain work experience in areas such as carpentry, hotel operations, and auto body repair. Other co-op students gain experience in areas such as journalism and agriculture.

Northeastern University, located in the heart of Boston, Massachusetts, is a leader in cooperative education. Many students who participate in the program earn their degree in five years. After completing their freshman year, students alternate work and studies for four years. Northeastern uses a quarter-term calendar. Therefore, each year students have two terms of courses and two terms of work. Work opportunities are not limited to the Boston area. In fact, students have both national and international opportunities.

If you participate in a co-op program, you may find you need more time than others to complete your graduation requirements. Of course, you can also work separately from your studies.

In co-op programs, employers coordinate their hiring with the college. You gain experience that will help you more fully develop job skills, often in your chosen field. This experience will also help you find work after you graduate. In many cases, you may even have a job already waiting for you with an employer that hired you through the co-op program.

What are internships? Like co-op programs, internships enable you to apply what you have learned in your courses to the workplace. They allow you to combine the spirit of independent study with the practical experience you can gain from cooperative learning.

Colleges that offer internship programs usually allow you to apply your internship toward your graduation requirements.

Interns are supervised by someone at their place of work. However, they are also guided by faculty members to make sure that academic goals are being met.

Students often arrange their own internships. In addition, many companies offer internships to college students. For instance, computer science students at the University of Pittsburgh have had opportunities to work with firms such as Alcoa, IBM, Mellon National Bank, and Westinghouse. At George Washington University, some interns work at the White House or on Capitol Hill.

Some internships are paid. Many, especially those with nonprofit organizations, are not. In either case, you gain direct experience, make progress toward your degree, and develop job contacts.

Dale Murphy is a criminal justice major at the University of Maryland. He was recently an intern at the Bureau of Justice Statistics, the U.S. agency that gathers and analyzes information about crime. Dale also plans to be an intern with a local sheriff's department.

Ideas for Internships

Broadcast. Work for a television station; conduct research for news stories or special features; learn how television programs are made.

Government. Work on a candidate's campaign; help research issues, organize volunteers, publicize rallies, schedule special events, and answer questions from the media.

Business Administration. Help a company research how consumers are reacting to one of its products; develop a survey, gather information, analyze responses to the survey, summarize findings, make a report to the company's management about the results.

Performing Arts. Work with a community chorus; research and write grant proposals; coordinate transportation and other behind-the-scenes efforts; publicize concerts; help develop long-term plan.

LIBRARIES AND LEARNING CENTERS

If you think that a library is just a place where they keep a lot of books and magazines, think again! College libraries have many resources that can be of great help to you. At many colleges, the library is part of an even larger learning center that offers special services to students.

College libraries can have hundreds of thousands, even millions, of books, periodicals, and other resources!

Most colleges have a central library where books, magazines, and other resources are housed. Many colleges have other libraries that focus on a certain field of study. For example, music and art departments often have libraries where recordings and art prints are available.

Spaces and Places at the Library

Main Desk. Command central for the library. If you don't know where to go, or how to use the library, start here!

Catalog. Lists all books, periodicals, and other resources available at the library; many catalogs are now computerized; some colleges have card catalogs with information stored on index cards.

Circulation Desk. Where you check out books and resources that can be taken out of the library (resources that circulate); librarians can help with inter-library loans—borrowing materials from other libraries.

Reference Desk. Atlases, maps, encyclopedias, yearbooks, special guides, and other research materials are here, but cannot be checked out.

Periodicals. Magazines, newspapers, and journals (dated resources that are published periodically) are found here; some can be checked out; many stored on microfilm or microfiche—can be viewed on a screen.

Stacks. Shelves where books are stored; sometimes open to students.

Dartmouth College has nine libraries that specialize in areas such as music, art, and biomedical sciences. Together, the libraries have over 2 million books, 20,000 periodicals, 160,000 maps, and 2.3 million items on microfiche. All of these resources are listed in a computerized catalog that is available throughout the world!

Some libraries also have collections of works by local authors.

What are special collections? Libraries are important centers for research. Many libraries have collections of materials on specialized subjects. These special collections help the college attract outstanding scholars to teach, to research, and to study. For instance, the University of New Mexico in Albuquerque houses the Center for Southwest Research. The Center's collections emphasize southwestern music and architecture, and books on the American West. In the Chapin Library of Rare Books at Williams College in Massachusetts, you can find official copies of the Bill of Rights, the Declaration of Independence, the Constitution, and the Articles of Confederation—an impressive combination!

Colleges are often called ivory towers, a name that comes from the look of many college libraries. Colby College's Miller Library, in Waterville, Maine, provides the classic image of an ivory tower. At night, the blue light that shines near the top of the tower can be seen from miles away.

Computer labs. Most colleges have rooms with computers set up for student use. These labs are especially important to students who do not have their own computers. Here you can develop spreadsheets, write programs, and work on other assignments. You can use other software that will help you in your classes.

A growing number of computer labs provide students with access to the Internet.

Computer labs may let you connect to the college's mainframe computer, helping you with larger projects. Social science students, for example, may have thousands of complicated surveys to analyze. They would need the computer power they can get through a computer lab.

Audio-Visual (A-V) centers. Most libraries have audio and video equipment for student use. You may be required to watch a documentary film, study some slides, or listen to a political speech. The A-V center provides you with access to these materials. Other times you need to use equipment to make an audio recording, shoot and edit a videotape, or take photographs for a presentation. Again, the A-V center can assist you.

Language and listening labs. Students who are learning to speak foreign languages practice out of the classroom. You can develop your skills in language labs. Here you borrow audiotapes or compact discs (CDs) and then listen to recorded material. You might practice repeating phrases and conversations or answer questions about what you have heard. Many labs have software programs that help you build grammar and vocabulary skills. Films and videos are also available.

Writing centers. The ability to communicate clearly is extremely important. But many students arrive at college without the writing skills they will need to succeed in college and beyond.

In recent years, many colleges have established writing centers. These centers are designed to help you with your writing, not only for English classes, but for all classes. The faculty members and staff at the writing centers can work with you on basic grammar skills. They can also help you learn to develop a comfortable style, organize your thoughts, present logical arguments, and develop a plan for writing a research paper. Even students who write well may need help organizing and preparing a research paper.

Tutoring. Many students, regardless of their overall ability, find they need extra help with certain courses. Most colleges have programs where these students can get one-on-one help from a tutor. Tutors may be faculty members, staff, graduate students, and sometimes even other students.

In many cases, tutoring is provided free of charge to students who need extra help.

STUDENTS WITH SPECIAL NEEDS

Most colleges provide services for students with special needs. These services contribute to student success, enabling students to participate fully in campus life.

Physical and learning disabilities. Passage of the Americans with Disabilities Act resulted in many changes. Some, such as elevators and ramps, handicapped parking spaces, and wheelchair access, help people get to class and other activities. Other changes help students to have the same learning opportunities as their classmates.

Colleges help students who are blind get audiotaped and Braille versions of books. They can provide readers, writers, and interpreters to help students who need these services. They may even be able to help students with transportation, class location, and special testing arrangements.

Many colleges have programs that help students who are the first in their family to go to college. Other programs address the needs of older students.

Other challenges. Students can face a variety of other challenges. For some students, English is not their first or native language. Many colleges offer English as a Second Language (ESL) programs to help them overcome language barriers. Whatever challenges you face, check whether a college has the services you need to succeed.

Gallaudet University in Washington, D.C., is the leading college for hearing-impaired students. Founded in 1864, the university has over 1,500 undergraduate students and more than 300 graduate students. Gallaudet's library has the world's largest collection of deafness-related resources.

LEARNING ASSISTANCE

Many students just need help getting started. Most colleges have special training sessions to help you increase your reading speed, take effective notes, organize your time, improve your study habits, prepare for exams, write research papers, and use computers. Colleges also have programs that help you become familiar with important places and services on campus. Campus publications, the advising center, and the library can tell you more.

 ## LEARNING MATERIALS

In addition to attending classes in many different settings, you will use several types of learning materials in college.

In many courses, you will be assigned several shorter, but more focused books to read. For example, in an American government class, you may read specialized books about the presidency, the Constitution, the legislature, the courts, power, and the media.

The learning tools you will probably use most often in college are books. Many textbooks are similar to the ones you use in school now. Their level is higher, but they have built-in aids to help you learn the subject: exercises, illustrations and photos, tables and charts, chapter reviews, and more. For many courses you will be assigned one book. Some books, like a calculus book, may be used for more than one term.

Because so much learning is now taking place on computers, many books now come with software. The software may be in diskette or CD form or it may be available directly on-line through your computer.

There is one thing you count on. As technology continues to develop, the different ways you can learn at college will continue to grow.

Other Learning Materials

Study Guides	Chapter reviews, summaries, sample quizzes and tests, and glossaries.
Solutions Manuals	Detailed solutions to exercises in the book; used a lot in math and science courses.
Notes	Professor's class notes available through library or bookstore; can help you prepare for or follow up on classroom lectures.
Exams	Exams from earlier years kept on file for your review when preparing for tests.
Lab Kits	Supplies used in laboratory sessions, for example, safety glasses or dissecting kit.
Studio Kits	Art supplies, including charcoal, crayons, drawing pencils, paints, and drawing pads.
Audiotapes	May be reviews of lectures; also used in foreign language classes for drill or practice.
Videotapes	May supplement textbook; sometimes interactive; may also be copy of lectures for students who miss class.
Computer Practice	Often a computerized version of a study guide, giving you extra practice and drill on selected topics.
Simulations	May be computerized; gives opportunity to test real situations, e.g., business simulation may let you pretend to run a company.
CD-ROM	Combines study guides, audiotapes, and videotapes into one computerized format.

7

HOW DO I GATHER INFORMATION?

Choosing a college is like choosing clothes to wear for a special occasion. The trick is finding something that looks good on you *and* fits well. Just because it's the right fit for someone else doesn't mean it's right for you.

Before you can choose a college, you need to learn as much as possible about the options that are available to you. You can find out about individual colleges from many different sources.

In this chapter, we will look at ways to gather information. Then you can begin to compare colleges and find one that is right for you.

Information: There's Lots of It!

You just need to know where to look and what to ask. People, libraries, books, computer programs, multimedia materials, and the colleges themselves are all important sources of information.

You don't have to go very far to start gathering information. And it may take you a little while to decide what to ask. You may even have to go back to some sources more than once with follow-up questions. But that's o.k.

The questions you might ask are similar to questions you would ask people about careers (see Chapter 2).

Most people are happy to help someone who is curious and interested in college. Never be shy about asking for help.

Who Can Tell You More About College?

Family. Did your parents go to college? How about brothers or sisters? Perhaps you can talk with an uncle, aunt, or cousins who have gone.

Friends and Neighbors. Have you ever talked about college with your friends? Are any of them thinking about going? Perhaps they have older brothers or sisters who go to college or are applying. Do you mow the lawn, babysit, or run errands for neighbors? Find out if any of them have gone to college and ask their advice.

Teachers. Your teachers have all gone to college. Choose a couple with whom you are close or whose opinion you really value. Ask them.

Counselors. Ask your guidance counselors at school for help. They might be especially helpful suggesting ways to find out more. They can show you important materials in your school.

Others. Do not forget members of your church or synagogue, your doctor, camp counselor, or anyone else who comes to mind!

Libraries. The librarians at both your school and public libraries are important allies as you gather information. While anyone at the library can be of help, you may want to start with the reference librarians. They can show you how to locate many important materials.

What kind of books are available? If you go into almost any bookstore, you will find dozens of books on almost every topic having to do with college. In fact, many bookstores have entire sections devoted to books about college.

You will find guides that describe every college in the country. Some are based on information from the colleges. Others give you information from students. Some books rate colleges based on the best value for your money, the best colleges for women, the best programs in a major, and so forth. Other guides look at topics such as getting into college and saving or raising money.

You may also find special companies that can help you in your search for colleges.

Is this information available in other ways? You can find software and CD programs that have similar information. You may also have access to on-line services. In addition, you may be able to get videotapes from the colleges themselves, your library, or even your local video store.

Information is available through the Internet. Several major guides are on-line, allowing you to conduct a computerized search for colleges. Many colleges have home pages—locations on the Internet where you can learn more about the college, see pictures, and write to people on campus. In coming years, college videos will be available through the computer.

What information do colleges provide? You will find that colleges provide information in many ways. The most traditional way has been through printed materials such as catalogs and viewbooks. In addition, college representatives visit students at high schools and at college fairs. Colleges also encourage students to visit their campuses whenever possible.

While all of these sources are helpful, you should always try to visit the colleges in which you are most interested.

Today's technology enables colleges to offer you information in more ways then ever before. The combination of videotapes, software, and the Internet enables you to visit a campus without ever leaving home.

Technology also expands your ability to contact colleges. Now, in addition to using mail and the telephone, you can use electronic mail (e-mail) when you contact colleges for information. You can use a computer to send your request for information to a specific office. And in many cases, you can even send in your application through the computer!

Some college representatives are college recruiters. Their job is not only to answer questions that students have, but also to find and encourage eligible students to apply to their college. The information you get from recruiters is almost always on target. However, listen more closely to what recruiters have to say about the colleges they represent, not to what they tell you about other colleges.

When you contact the college admissions office, you are letting them know you are interested in the college. The office may add you to its mailing list so that you will receive up-to-date news that might help you when you apply.

On the next page, you will find a description of the various sources of information that colleges provide. On the page after that, you will find a sample letter you could send to an admissions office in order to get more information. Many college guides provide addresses for admissions offices across the country.

Colleges Provide Information in Different Ways

Viewbook. May be called a bulletin; overview booklet that provides general information about the college, usually with photographs; helps you decide if you want to learn more about the college.

Catalog. Detailed book for students; describes requirements for graduation and majors; lists and describes courses; explains college's rules and regulations; some colleges may charge a small fee.

Videotapes. Visual introduction to the college; overview similar to that of viewbook; often gives chance to hear student points of view; some colleges provide videos to keep, others charge small fee or loan them; often available through high school guidance offices and libraries.

College Fair. Event at which many colleges set up information booths; often sponsored by high schools or school districts; you can visit booths, talk with a college representative, pick up viewbooks and other printed material; you can place your name on a mailing list for information; college representatives may work for the college (e.g., college recruiter) or may be a volunteer (e.g., alumni).

High School Visits. College representatives visit high schools, usually in fall; students sign up through guidance office to meet with college representatives; some colleges schedule sessions for many schools.

Electronic Information. Increasingly popular way to send and receive information; many colleges have home pages on the Internet; also, many colleges correspond with students by e-mail (see pages 130-131).

Campus Tours and Open Houses. Chance to see the college in person; tours available year-round, often conducted by students; open houses, other programs available several times, especially in fall; visitors ask questions, tour campus, meet faculty, students, and others.

Interview. On-campus with admissions counselor or off-campus (often with alumni member); opportunity for you and college to get to know each other better.

Write to a College!

This letter could be sent to the admissions office or to the chairperson of an academic department. It can also be sent electronically, if you have the e-mail address. Whenever possible, address your letter to a specific person.

[current date]

Frederic Siegel
Director of Admissions*
George Washington University
Washington, D.C. 20052

Dear Mr. Siegel:

I am a twelve-year-old student and attend the sixth grade at Bayside Middle School in Anytown, State. I know that I will not be going to college for a while, but I am starting to think about it. I am interested in learning as much as I can.

I would like to know more about George Washington University. Could you please send me a viewbook and any other materials you think would be useful for me? I am especially interested in computers and would like to know if you have any computer classes for students my age.

My address is:

Sandy Brown
987 Main Street
Anytown, State 55555

Thank you very much for your help.

Sincerely,

Sandy Brown

Many college guides list the names of the directors or deans of admissions along with their mailing addresses. You will probably start seeing more e-mail addresses as well.

SPECIAL PROGRAMS

Your guidance counselor may be able to give you more information about summer programs, as can the colleges. You can also find specialized guides describing summer programs across the country.

Some colleges offer special programs to introduce students to the campus. Most of these programs are for high school students, although some are designed for younger students as well.

Many colleges offer summer learning programs. Some focus on specific topics such as computers, astronomy, and journalism. Some programs are for minority students, some are for kids interested in science, and others are for students with learning disabilities. The programs may be similar to summer camp. You may even have the chance to live on campus for a couple of weeks.

For the past several years, the University of Texas at El Paso (UTEP) has run the Mother-Daughter Program. This special program is designed especially to encourage young Hispanic girls and their mothers to see college as part of their future. The program begins in sixth grade. Teams of mothers and daughters meet one Saturday each month to participate in activities dealing with academic, personal, career, and community-life issues. During the year, the mothers and daughters tour the campus and meet with successful Hispanic female students. They participate in a career day, meeting with Hispanic women who have developed successful professional careers. The teams participate in a leadership conference, where they take on community service projects. The girls also take part in summer camp, staying on campus for two weeks. The program does not end with sixth grade: Follow-up activities take place all the way through high school graduation.

☛ WHAT DO YOU NEED TO KNOW?

The United States has thousands of colleges! How can you choose among them? Start by understanding their characteristics. You will then be able to compare different colleges without any difficulty.

College guides define size in different ways. Be sure to check how they measure size. You can also check the actual number of students.

Size. The number of students a college has is its size. A college's overall size can affect class size, social life, availability of courses and resources, the range of activities, and your ability to participate in them.

Location. Location refers to where a college is. It does not refer simply to city and state. For example, is the college close to home or far away? Is the college near an airport, train station, or bus station? How do you get to it? Is the college near anyone you know? Is the weather warm or cold, rainy or dry? What activities are near the college (museums, sports events, hiking, and so forth)?

Setting. A college's immediate surroundings makes up its setting. College settings are usually described as urban, suburban, small town, and rural. Setting also refers to the campus. Does the campus have a lake or a pond? Is it flat or hilly? Is it wooded? What style is its architecture?

You can even look at setting in terms of how the campus is laid out. Is the campus big or small? Is the campus spread out or are the buildings close together? How far are the classroom buildings and the library from student housing or the parking lots? How long would it take to get from a dining hall to a classroom building? Where are the places to relax and the places to socialize?

College Size and Settings

The first college listed for each category is a four-year college. The second college listed is a two-year college.

Size*	Setting	College or University
Small	Urban	Agnes Scott College (GA)
		Maria College (NY)
Small	Suburban	Alaska Pacific University (AK)
		Maryland College of Art and Design
Small	Rural/Small Town	University of the Ozarks (AR)
		Lamar Community College (CO)
Medium	Urban	Augustana College (IL)
		Galveston College (TX)
Medium	Suburban	Rollins College (FL)
		Berkshire Community College (MA)
Medium	Rural/Small Town	Middlebury College (VT)
		Lenoir Community College (NC)
Large	Urban	Drake University (IA)
		Spokane Community College (WA)
Large	Suburban	Washington University (MO)
		Clackamas Community College (OR)
Large	Rural/Small Town	University of South Dakota (SD)
		Ocean County College (NJ)
Very Large	Urban	Temple University (PA)
		Jefferson Community College (KY)
Very Large	Suburban	Arizona State University (AZ)
		Oakland Community College (MI)
Very Large	Rural/Small Town	Auburn University (AL)
		Butte College (CA)

*In this chart:
Small   under 1,000 students
Medium   1,000 to 5,000 students
Large   5,000 to 10,000 students
Very large over 10,000 students

The cost of going to college is important. But do not let cost restrict where you apply to college.

Cost. College costs vary quite a lot. Whether you attend a two-year or a four-year college affects your costs as do other factors (e.g., public college or private college). In Chapters 10 and 11, we will look more closely at college costs and ways to pay for college.

The United States is unique when it comes to college opportunities. People who really want to go to college can have that opportunity. They can be helped with costs in many ways.

Financial assistance. Your family can provide a certain amount of help paying for college. Other forms of assistance are also available through loans, scholarships (money that you do not need to repay), and jobs. Some colleges can offer more support than others. *Whether you can afford a particular college depends on more than its costs. Your true cost is also based on how much assistance you receive.* As you gather information, try to learn how many students receive assistance from the colleges in which you are interested as well as how much support they receive.

Ohio State University offers 170 majors and almost 11,000 courses!

Available majors. Most colleges, especially large universities, offer many academic programs. Some specialize in areas such as performing arts, religious studies, culinary arts, and technology. Colleges have different strengths. For instance, Northwestern University's journalism program is one of its best. It is also one of the top journalism programs in the country.

Colleges often have strengths within fields of study. For example, a particular college may have a top psychology program, with a special strength in experimental psychology, which is research-oriented. However, that college may not offer much in clinical psychology, which is oriented toward patients. If your interest is in the clinical areas, you may need to look elsewhere.

Academic opportunity. In addition to knowing what programs a college offers, you want to know how hard it is to get into those programs. At many colleges, once you are accepted, you can major in whatever area you want. However, some areas of study, like engineering and nursing, may be limited to a certain number of students. Therefore, checking any restrictions a college may have on your favorite program is a very important part of gathering information.

> *Suppose Boston University is your school of choice and physical therapy your field of choice. Being accepted at Boston University does not automatically mean you can get into their physical therapy program. Only a limited number of students are accepted into the physical therapy program.*

In theory, at colleges with lower student-faculty ratios, professors have more time to spend with each student. A 13:1 ratio is lower than a 22:1 ratio.

Student-faculty ratio. A relatively easy piece of information to find is the number of students at a college for each faculty member. For example, a college with a student-faculty ratio of 13 to 1 (or 13:1) has thirteen students for each faculty member. This ratio is often used to indicate the opportunities that students have to interact with their professors. At a college with a 13:1 student-faculty ratio, you are likely to have more access to professors than at a college with a 22:1 ratio.

Faculty. Find out how many faculty members a college has, but ask other questions. How many have advanced degrees? Are most classes taught by full-time professors, by their assistants, or by part-time faculty? Who has received research, writing, or teaching awards? Do any particular departments dominate such awards? Are any of the departments recognized nationally?

Class Size. Your learning experience will vary depending on how many students are in your classes. Teaching methods and class size often go together. A class of 300 students limits the amount of interaction with the professor. Learn the average number of students in a typical class. Also try to find out the range of class size. How many classes have more than 50 students or fewer than 20 students? Which size do you prefer?

> *At Bryn Mawr College in Pennsylvania, very few classes have more than 50 students in them. And three out of every four classes have no more than 20 students in them. Bryn Mawr's student-faculty ratio is 9:1, or nine students for every teacher. What does this mean? Bryn Mawr students have a lot of access to their professors.*

Accreditation. In order to drive a car, you must earn your license by showing the Department of Motor Vehicles that you meet a set of standards. In a similar way, a college earns its accreditation by showing it has met certain standards.

You should always check a college's accreditation. Most are listed in the college's catalog or in the standard college guides. Your opportunities for careers, graduate schools, and professional programs could be hurt if the college you attend does not meet approved standards.

One type of accreditation is the kind the college earns as a whole. The college shows that it meets standards for its educational program, the services it provides, and its facilities. Many colleges are accredited by regional organizations such as the Southern Association of Colleges and Schools. Colleges can also be accredited by organizations such as the New York Board of Regents or the American Association of Bible Colleges.

Departments also earn accreditation. For example, the American Chemical Society approves chemistry programs at individual colleges.

Facilities. The buildings and other facilities on the college campus are an important factor when you are comparing colleges.

Are the buildings in good shape? Are classrooms comfortable? If you are going to live on campus in a dormitory, how big are the rooms? How close to the classroom buildings are they? How are the heating and air conditioning systems throughout the campus?

Is the library up to date? How crowded is it? Does it have comfortable chairs for the times you study there? How many books and periodicals does it have? Do science labs have modern equipment? Is the college as a whole wired for computers? Are computers available?

If you need or prefer a special diet, you might check if the food service on campus can meet your needs.

What are the athletic facilities like? How many dining halls are there and where are they located? Where is the student union (a center of activity for students) located and what facilities does it have? All these questions and more are part of judging a college's facilities.

Health facilities. Very often, health facilities get overlooked when students are comparing colleges. Learn what facilities are on campus in case you get sick or have health concerns such as asthma or diabetes. Is a medical staff available 24 hours a day? What kind of health insurance does the college offer? Where are hospitals located? (Are there any hospitals on campus?) Does the college charge for health care services? If so, how much?

Laws now require colleges to report information each year about the safety of their campuses. This information is available to anyone who asks for it.

Security. Try to learn about a college's safety record. How much crime, and what kind, takes place on campus? Is the college well lit at night? Does the college have an escort service to walk students across campus, if needed? Does the college have its own security force? How easy is it to reach them? Are emergency phones readily available if you need to dial for help? How well protected is the parking lot? How secure are the buildings where students live?

Do you plan to have a bike on campus? Find out where you can keep it secure.

Transportation. If you plan to live on campus, you might have questions about how easy it is to get from campus to nearby shopping, entertainment, or airports. Does the college provide local buses or other transportation? Are parking spaces available to students who live on campus?

If you plan to commute, you will also want to know about public transportation and parking spaces. You may want to know how close buses or trains come to campus, how often they run, what hours they run, and how much they cost. If you plan to drive, you may want to know how much parking permits cost and how far away the parking lots are from the classrooms, the library, and any other facilities you would regularly use.

Diversity measures the range of people's backgrounds: age, gender, geography, race, ethnicity, religion, and so forth.

Some students can use geography to their advantage for getting into certain colleges. For example, being from North Dakota may not help you get into a college in nearby Minnesota. However, it may help you get into a New England college looking for a national mix of students.

Do not assume that a college affiliated with a religious group only accepts students from that religion.

Diversity. College provides you with a unique opportunity to interact closely with people whose experiences and outlook are different from your own. Many colleges try to make sure that their students represent the diversity of our population.

The diversity of students at many public colleges tends to be similar to the diversity of the nearby population. Many community colleges draw on a small geographic area; students come from the nearby community. Other colleges are regional. Their students may include those from nearby states. Other colleges are national. They attract students from all over the United States and, in many cases, all over the world.

Colleges vary in the racial, ethnic, and gender mix of their students. Sometimes the racial and ethnic mix reflects the local population. For example, a higher number of people of Hispanic origin live in the southwest United States. Not surprisingly, colleges in the southwest tend to have a higher percentage of Hispanic students than colleges in other areas. Some colleges try to attract a broad diversity of students. Others serve specific groups of students. For example, Spelman College in Georgia is built around students who are not only African-American, but also female. Similarly, Morehouse College in Georgia is geared mostly toward African-American males.

Religious diversity at colleges also varies. Some colleges aim for a broad mix of backgrounds. Other colleges are more likely to have students with similar religious backgrounds, especially if the colleges are formally affiliated with a particular religious group.

Many colleges have organizations on campus that bring together students, faculty, staff, and members of the community to share religious and social activities. Three organizations found at many colleges are Newman (Catholic), Canterbury (Episcopalian), and Hillel (Jewish).

Religion. You may have questions about religious observances while you are at college. If answers are not in the college materials, ask an admissions counselor. Many colleges have interfaith chapels serving many denominations. They may also have advisors for specific religious groups. You may want to know if services for your own faith are held on campus or in the community. You may have certain dietary needs. For instance, if you are Islamic or Jewish, you may want to know about the availability of kosher foods. If you are neither Christian nor Jewish, you may want to learn about arrangements the college has to honor your needs for other observances and holidays.

The earlier you let the college know about any special services you need, the more easily the college can work with you to provide them.

Students with special needs. Some colleges have extensive services to help students who have disabilities and other special needs. If you are disabled or have other special needs or concerns, get the information you need early on about how the college can help you. Most colleges have offices or counselors who can work with you to solve or prevent problems. Many colleges provide help for students whose first language is not English. Other factors are important as well. For example, students who have learning disabilities may prefer small classes.

Many students are the first person in their family to attend college. These first-generation college students do not have physical or learning disabilities. But they may have special needs because they have no one in their family who can tell them what college is like. They may feel that they are less prepared than other students. Colleges often have programs to address the special concerns of first-generation students.

Challenge and Reputation. Some colleges are harder than other colleges. Courses are tougher, workload is heavier, and competition is fiercer. One way to judge the difficulty of a course is to look at the skill level needed for taking the course. Some physics courses, for example, require students to have algebra skills in order to handle the math portion of the course. But other physics courses require students to have calculus skills, a higher level of math. A college where most students take calculus-based physics is generally more difficult than one where most students take algebra-based physics.

A college's level of challenge is often a matter of opinion. But there are ways to measure a college's level of difficulty and its overall reputation.

One way is to look at a college's *selectivity*, which, in part, measures the academic record of students who enter the college. Looking at what students do after they graduate is also informative. How many graduates of a four-year college continue on for advanced degrees? How many graduates of a two-year college go on to four-year colleges?

In any rating guide, you need to understand the factors used to establish the rating. For example, are the ratings based on the author's personal opinion or are specific facts used?

Several magazines and guides that rate colleges are available. Some rate the overall college, taking into account many of the factors listed in this chapter. Others rate colleges more specifically, often by department. For example, you might be able to find a listing of the ten best economics departments in the country or colleges with the highest percentage of students going on to medical school. Talking to people is also an important way to learn about a college. Talk to graduates, students, teachers, counselors, and others.

Student activities. Learn what you can about the different activities available for students. What clubs does the college have? Do many guest speakers and performers come to the college?

What opportunities does the college have for you to get involved? Will you be able to act in a play or sing in a chorus? Will you be able to be active with student government? If you like to camp or participate in debates, will you be able to pursue these activities? Can you become active with a college newspaper or other publication?

If you like sports, will you be able to play with a college-sponsored team? Are there intramural sports available? If you are interested in a specific sport, such as rugby or cross country skiing, will you be able to follow up on that interest?

Campus activities provide a great way for students who commute to stay connected to the college.

Answers to many of these questions can be found in college viewbooks and newspapers, alumni magazines, and various college guides, especially those that include information that comes from students who are currently attending college.

Overall feeling for the college. Some colleges may not feel right to you no matter how many strengths they have. Others have weaknesses but still feel right to you. At some point ask yourself: What is my gut reaction to the college? Does it feel like a place where I would like to be? You may receive lots of advice from others and, in some cases, pressure to go one place or another. Certainly the views of others are important. But at some point you must listen to your own inner voice and whether it says to you, "This college will be great for me!"

8

WHERE SHOULD I APPLY?

Gathering information about colleges is a great starting point. In fact, you will probably collect more information than you can imagine! Your next important step is to figure out what matters most to you. Then you can zero in on certain colleges.

Will you find one college that is perfect for you? Maybe. But you will find that some colleges have advantages for you that others do not. If you know what is most important to you, choosing the right colleges will be much easier. This chapter will help you ask and answer the right questions about yourself and colleges. Learn how to do this and you will be well on your way to deciding where to apply!

KNOW YOURSELF

This process of evaluating yourself is often referred to as self-assessment.

Before you really begin to decide where to apply to college, take time to think about yourself. Think about your goals, your likes and dislikes, your abilities, and your resources.

What are your goals? Think about what you would like your life to be like when you are older. Do you have special interests that may affect the kind of career you will want someday? If you have a particular career in mind, then you should look for colleges that can help you reach that goal.

What do you do if your goals seem to conflict? Try to find colleges where you can pursue both goals—and have the time to explore and decide.

Perhaps you only have a general idea about your future. For example, travelling, living in a certain place, earning a lot of money, or helping your community may be very important to you—even though you're not sure how to accomplish any of these goals.

College provides wonderful opportunities for people less sure about their goals. You can test the waters and try out new directions. You can take courses in different areas. If you like, you can then pursue those new directions or try still other opportunities.

Don't be concerned or feel pressured if you are not sure what your goals are. College is not only for people with clear goals in sight. Most people find that their goals change throughout life. Knowing yourself does not mean that you must have all the answers about your future. However, if you have an understanding about how certain you are about your goals, you will be able to make better decisions about where to apply to college.

Through her years as a figure skater, world champion and Olympic medalist Debi Thomas never lost sight of her long-term goal to be a doctor. While skating, she attended Stanford University in California. After skating professionally, she continued her studies—attending medical school at Northwestern University in Illinois and always keeping her goals in focus.

What are your likes and dislikes? Your personal preferences about many things are important to your decisions about college. Would you rather live in a big city or a small town? What kind of weather do you prefer? Do you like being around lots of other people or do you prefer to spend time with one or two close friends? Do you want to go away from home—and if so, how far away? Would you rather live at or near home when you go to college? These and other questions are important when you decide where to apply. Being honest with yourself matters!

What are your abilities? Consider your strengths and weaknesses. Are you a good student? Does studying come easily to you? If the answers to these questions are "no," don't be discouraged. Just be realistic about how challenging a college you should consider. Do you have a knack for science or math? Does writing come easily to you? These kinds of questions might help lead you to areas of study and, in turn, to certain colleges.

In Chapter 14, we will look at steps that you can take between now and the time you apply to college.

If you know your abilities, then you will be able to work with them. You will be able to build on the strengths you have identified. You will also be able to take steps that can help you overcome or work with any weaknesses.

We will look at college costs and how to pay for college in Chapters 10 and 11.

What are your resources? At some point, you need to consider how you and your family will pay for college. You may not have answers yet. But never let cost keep you from applying to a college that is right for you in every other way.

You can meet college expenses in many ways. Financial support often comes from the college itself, or from companies, other organizations, and other family members. You may be surprised when you realize how many kinds of help are available. In fact, you may be able to help too!

Still, you need to be realistic about what you and your family can afford. As you make your list of colleges that interest you, take note of those that are more affordable and those for which you would need to get extra help.

Many students work while they earn an associate degree. They then transfer to a four-year college and attend it full-time for two years while earning a bachelor's degree.

Will you have to work while you go to college? If you have a good job, you may decide that going to college close to home or part-time makes the most sense. Perhaps you can afford to be a full-time student for two years, but not four years. The best decision may be to earn an associate degree at a two-year school. Then you can work while continuing your education.

Resources can affect your choices in other ways. For example, if you plan to live at home, will you have a car or access to public transportation?

Some government agencies have programs to help students with college. For example, the National Security Agency (NSA) may pay for college if you work for it during summers and a certain number of years after graduating.

It's What You Think that Matters!

Your Goals:

What subjects interest me?
Do I want to continue my education after high school?
What do I want to be?
Do I need to go to college for this career?

Your Likes and Dislikes:

Do I want to live away from home? If so, how far away?
How important is it that friends go to the same college I attend?
Am I comfortable around a lot of people at one time?
Do I want to be with different kinds of people or people just like me?
Would I prefer a city, the suburbs, small towns, or rural areas?
What kind of weather do I like or does it matter to me?
Do I have any special needs or concerns (religious, medical, etc.)?
Which activities are most important to me (arts, sports, clubs, etc.)?
Do I want to play sports when I'm at college?
Which special opportunities are important to me (study abroad,
    independent study, exchange programs)?

Your Abilities:

What kind of a student am I?
What are my strongest subjects?
What are my weakest subjects?
How are my study skills?
How well do I handle competition and pressure?

Your Resources:

Are there limits to what I can pay for college?
Will my family be able to help me?
Can I go to college full-time if I want?
How will I get to classes (live on campus, drive, public transportation, etc.)?

■☞ BUILD A LIST

You may ask how knowing about yourself helps you figure out where you should apply to college. That's a fair question! Let's see how it works.

Suppose you live in San Diego, but hear interesting things about Davidson College in North Carolina. You should first ask how you feel about going to college on the East Coast, so far from home. If that idea is o.k. with you, start exploring Davidson more. If you don't want to go that far away, don't add Davidson to your list.

Start by building a list of colleges. You can build your list in a couple of different ways. First, you can keep a list of colleges as you hear about them. Some may be colleges near where you live. Some may be colleges where family and friends have gone. Still others will catch your interest after watching a game on television, hearing about where a famous person went to college, or even reading about an important event that took place at a college.

Learn more about these colleges. Use college guides, software programs, and the World Wide Web. Don't forget to talk to people who may be familiar with these colleges. Decide whether what you have learned is of interest. In short, decide whether to keep the college on your list.

Again, suppose you live in San Diego and know that you don't want to be too far from home. Start by looking at colleges in Southern California and Arizona.

Another way to build a list is to ask the questions described earlier in the chapter. Decide what is important to you—then look for a college that matches your priorities. If a college matches the things that matter most to you, add it to your list. This approach is a more focused one, but you may overlook some unexpected opportunities.

Few colleges will have everything that you want. But, in all likelihood, several will have many of the qualities that matter most to you. And with this list in hand, you can start "zooming in" on this group of colleges.

How can I use my computer to build my list?
If you have access to a computer with a modem, then you have a valuable tool that can help you build your list. You can use the computer to "surf the Internet," learning more about colleges.

Most home pages are found through the World Wide Web (WWW), often called the Web. The Web provides a way of finding your way around the Internet. It also provides a visual approach so that you can see photographs and graphics.

Many colleges have home pages on the Internet and the number keeps growing. A home page is a location on the Internet which you can reach in several ways. Each location has its own address. Once you're in the Internet, you can reach a college's home page by typing in its address.

Each home page is different. Many have photos of the college. Most provide basic information, including a description of the fields of study and advice about applying. Some home pages list the faculty—you may even get to see their pictures. You might learn about campus events or read the student newspaper on-line. Your school's computer specialist or your counselor should be able to help you find out more about colleges on the Internet.

You may have access to several tools that help you search the World Wide Web. These tools are often called Web browsers. In many cases, you would type in the name of the college in which you are interested. The browser searches the Internet and comes back with a list of Internet addresses that are linked to that college name. From there, you can go to one of those addresses (some will be college home pages). Yahoo and Lycos are two of many systems that search the Internet. If the company that provides you with access to the Internet also has access to Yahoo and Lycos, then you can use them to help you learn more about specific colleges.

College Home Pages on the Web

State	College or University	Web Address
Alabama	University of South Alabama	www.usouthal.edu
Alaska	University of Alaska	www.alaska.edu
Arizona	Scottsdale Community Coll.	www.sc.maricopa.edu
Arkansas	Harding University	www.harding.edu
California	San Diego State University	www.sdsu.edu
Colorado	Pueblo Community College	www.pcc.cccoes.edu
Connecticut	Trinity College	www.trincoll.edu
Delaware	University of Delaware	www.udel.edu
Florida	Brevard Community College	www.brevard.cc.fl.us
Georgia	Georgia State University	www.gsu.edu
Hawaii	Hawaii Pacific University	www.hpu.edu
Idaho	Idaho State University	www.isu.edu
Illinois	Bradley University	www.bradley.edu
Indiana	DePauw University	www.depauw.edu
Iowa	Upper Iowa University	www.uiu.edu
Kansas	Kansas State University	www.ksu.edu
Kentucky	Centre College	www.centre.edu
Louisiana	Tulane University	www.tulane.edu
Maine	Colby College	www.colby.edu
Maryland	Howard Community College	www.howardcc.edu
Massachusetts	Clark University	www.clarku.edu
Michigan	Kalamazoo College	www.kzoo.edu
Minnesota	Normandale Comm. College	www.nr.cc.mn.us
Mississippi	University of Mississippi	www.olemiss.edu
Missouri	Washington University	www.wustl.edu
Montana	University of Montana	www.umt.edu

The home pages listed here are on the World Wide Web. To find more four-year colleges, including some not on the Web, go to the following address:

www.clas.ufl.edu/CLAS/american-universities.html

Include the hyphen listed in this address.

College Home Pages on the Web

State	College or University	Web Address
Nebraska	Univ. of Nebraska—Omaha	www.unomaha.edu
Nevada	CC of Southern Nevada	www.ccsn.nevada.edu
New Hampshire	Plymouth State College	www.plymouth.edu
New Jersey	New Jersey Inst. of Tech.	www.njit.edu
New Mexico	New Mexico State Univ.	www.nmsu.edu
New York	Rensselaer Polytechnic Inst.	www.rpi.edu
North Carolina	Elon College	www.elon.edu
North Dakota	Dickinson State University	www.dsn.nodak.edu
Ohio	Case Western Reserve Univ.	www.cwru.edu
Oklahoma	University of Oklahoma	www.uoknor.edu
Oregon	Central Oregon Comm. Coll.	www.cocc.edu
Pennsylvania	Haverford College	www.haverford.edu
Rhode Island	Brown University	www.brown.edu
South Carolina	Greenville Technical College	www.gvltec.edu
South Dakota	Northern State University	www.northern.edu
Tennessee	University of Memphis	www.memphis.edu
Texas	Southern Methodist Univ.	www.smu.edu
Utah	University of Utah	www.utah.edu
Vermont	Middlebury College	www.middlebury.edu
Virginia	James Madison University	www.jmu.edu
Washington	Gonzaga University	www.gonzaga.edu
West Virginia	Marshall University	www.marshall.edu
Wisconsin	Marquette University	www.mu.edu
Wyoming	University of Wyoming	www.uwyo.edu
District of Columbia	American University	www.american.edu

A listing of many two-year colleges can be found at a different location than the listing for four-year colleges. Try looking for this listing under Community College Web at the following address:

www.mcli.dist.maricopa.edu/cc

Include the slash listed in this address.

FIND OUT MORE

You may find lots of reasons for visiting a college, for instance, attending an athletic event, a drama camp, a debate competition, or a graduation.

You can find out more information in many ways. And a lot of them are fun. For starters, whenever you can, visit college campuses. The colleges you visit don't have to be ones you want to attend. Any college you visit can give you ideas about different types of colleges.

If a college really interests you, try to visit it if at all possible. There is simply no better way to get a feel for the college. You can take a campus tour, usually with a student guide. You can see campus events or visit important places—the library, classrooms, the student union, and sometimes even the rooms where students live on campus.

While you can usually drop in on a college, try to call in advance whenever possible. Arrange to visit the admissions office if you can.

You can meet with members of the admissions office. Also, many colleges have visiting days called open houses. When you visit, you may also be able to speak with students and professors.

Even if you can't visit, you can go to a college fair and talk to a representative. You can write to the admissions office with your specific questions. You can also talk with alumni volunteers who are happy to meet students interested in the college they attended. They can share their experiences with you, answer some questions you have, and help you get answers to others.

Use your family vacations to visit colleges. Find out if any colleges are near where you will be travelling and visit them. For instance, if you are visiting Civil War battlesites, you may want to stop in at Gettysburg College in Pennsylvania.

Is Getting into College Hard?

As you decide where to apply, you should ask yourself "Can I get into this college?"

Colleges have different policies for deciding who can attend. They take many different factors into consideration. The way colleges select who may attend is often referred to as selectivity. Overall, when we look at a college's selectivity, we are looking at whether getting into the college is easy or difficult.

What are the different kinds of selectivity? For the most part, college selectivity falls into three categories: open admissions, selective admissions, and competitive admissions.

Open admissions. Open admissions colleges provide opportunities for students who may not get into other schools. At open admissions colleges, almost everyone who applies is accepted. Once you are admitted, your skills are evaluated. If you are ready for college-level classes, then you may take them. However, if you are not ready, you take developmental classes. These are classes designed to improve your academic and study skills.

Many open admissions colleges also offer courses taught at more challenging levels than regular college-level courses. These courses are often called honors courses. Sometimes entire programs are taught at an honors level.

Most community colleges have open admissions. In addition, several state colleges as well as some private colleges have open admissions.

Selective admissions. Colleges using selective admissions have clear requirements for admitting students. As long as there is space, students who meet these requirements are usually accepted. However, students who do not meet these requirements are not admitted. Also, in cases where there are limited spaces, if you apply too late, you risk not being admitted—even if you qualify.

Grade point average, class rank, and entrance exams are all discussed in Chapter 9.

Colleges often require you to have a certain grade point average or higher. For example, you may be required to have at least a B average in high school. Requirements can differ quite a bit. Some colleges look at class rank (how your academic performance compares to that of your classmates). Some look at scores on a required set of tests called entrance exams. Still others might look at the courses you have taken in high school.

Many college guides divide competitive admissions into levels such as highly competitive and most competitive. The guides will explain their levels. The levels are often based on the percentage of students who are accepted, as well as other requirements.

Competitive admissions. As with colleges that use selective admissions, colleges that use competitive admissions also have clear requirements for admitting students. These requirements are usually more strict.

Space at these colleges is limited. More students apply than can be accepted. Therefore, meeting the requirements for admission does not mean you will get in. Basically, students are competing with each other for the spaces.

Selective admissions are fairly objective. Colleges can measure applications in the exact same way. Competitive admissions are more subjective. Scores and averages matter, as do more personal factors—what others say about you, essays, your activities, and special talents.

How can I find out what is required? Finding out what colleges look for in their applications is easier than you might think. This information is available in many places. Among the easier ways to check are by reading guides that describe all the colleges and by talking with representatives from college admissions offices.

You should look for two kinds of information. First, find out what the colleges want to know about you. For instance, some colleges look closely at test scores, others do not. Second, learn what you can about the typical students entering the college. What are their grades? How do their grades compare with their classmates? How well did the students score on the entrance exams?

High school counselors often keep track of which students are admitted to certain colleges each year. They can give you a good sense of what qualifications are needed at many of these schools.

Many guides provide lists comparing colleges based on selectivity. You can find out quickly which colleges across the country are the most competitive and which have open admissions. The entries for each college will also give you more specific information about typical students.

Most colleges will look at special circumstances. For example, suppose your grades suffer one year because of illness or a lot of moving. If your grades had been strong before and they bounce back later, many colleges will take into account your circumstances.

Remember that most colleges want to have a fairly diverse student body. Many people immediately think of race, religion, geographical background, and economic background when they think of diversity. But most colleges also look at students' experiences when they look at diversity. Your own experiences in life may make up for other areas in which your qualifications are not as strong.

Do you need to be realistic about your academic achievement? Of course, but don't sell yourself short. If your qualifications are anywhere near what a college requires, do not rule it out.

Examples of Selectivity Across the States

State	College or University	Selectivity
Alabama	University of Alabama	selective
Alaska	University of Alaska—Fairbanks	selective
Arizona	Northern Arizona University	selective
Arkansas	Philander Smith College	open
California	Harvey Mudd College	competitive
Colorado	Colorado College	competitive
Connecticut	Charter Oak State College	open
Delaware	Wilmington College	open
Florida	Manatee Community College	open
Georgia	Emory University	competitive
Hawaii	Kauai Community College	open
Idaho	University of Idaho	selective
Illinois	University of Chicago	competitive
Indiana	University of Notre Dame	competitive
Iowa	Iowa State University	selective
Kansas	Kansas State University	open
Kentucky	Jefferson Community College	open
Louisiana	University of New Orleans	selective
Maine	Bowdoin College	competitive
Maryland	Towson State University	selective
Massachusetts	Mount Ida College	open
Michigan	Western Michigan University	selective
Minnesota	Carleton College	competitive
Mississippi	University of Mississippi	selective
Missouri	University of Missouri	selective
Montana	College of Great Falls	open

Most states offer a wide range of selectivity. Florida's colleges cover the full range. New College of the The University of South Florida is among the nation's most competitive colleges. Florida State University is one of Florida's selective colleges. And Edison Community College has open admissions.

Examples of Selectivity Across the States

State	College or University	Selectivity
Nebraska	Peru State College	open
Nevada	University of Nevada	selective
New Hampshire	Keene State College	selective
New Jersey	Union County College	open
New Mexico	New Mexico State University	selective
New York	Cooper Union	competitive
North Carolina	Duke University	competitive
North Dakota	Bismarck State College	open
Ohio	University of Toledo	open
Oklahoma	Rose State College	open
Oregon	Reed College	competitive
Pennsylvania	Millersville University	selective
Rhode Island	Brown University	competitive
South Carolina	Trident Technical College	open
South Dakota	Dakota State University	selective
Tennessee	Vanderbilt University	competitive
Texas	Rice University	competitive
Utah	Utah Valley State College	open
Vermont	University of Vermont	selective
Virginia	Washington and Lee University	competitive
Washington	Whitman College	competitive
West Virginia	West Liberty State College	selective
Wisconsin	Lawrence University	competitive
Wyoming	Sheridan College	open
District of Columbia	Georgetown University	competitive

Brown University, Columbia University, Cornell University, Dartmouth College, Harvard University, Princeton University, the University of Pennsylvania, and Yale University are among the nation's most competitive colleges. Together these colleges are called the Ivy League, named for the ivy that grows along the walls of their buildings.

NARROW THE FIELD

Visiting colleges and speaking with others can be a big help as you narrow your list.

When you first look at colleges, the choices can seem overwhelming! But when you think about the different factors—size, setting, academics, and many others—you can narrow your list quite a bit. If your list has more than fifteen colleges, you may want to narrow it more before you apply.

Many students who are unsure about where they will go find that a list of five to seven colleges covers most of their choices.

How many colleges should be on my final list? There's no magic number. If you plan to go to a community college or a state university, you may have only one or two colleges on your list. If you are certain you will be accepted, having so few on your list is fine. But if you have not made a final decision, think about your chances of being accepted at each college. Your final list should have a range of colleges on it, including at least one college where you know you'll be accepted.

Colleges where you know you will be accepted are called your safety schools.

Will I Be Accepted?

No Sweat. Have on your list one or more colleges where you know you will be accepted. Open admissions colleges may not have application deadlines, but apply to them early for special programs and financial support. You can include selective colleges on your "no sweat" list if you are certain you meet or exceed their admission requirements.

The Right Match. Include colleges that are your ideal choices and for which you are well-qualified. These include colleges for which you have what is needed to be accepted and succeed, although limited space may be a factor in your acceptance.

Reach Out. Include one or two colleges which you really like and where you meet or exceed many, if not all, the criteria for admission. If you do not get in, do not be too disappointed. But be willing to take at least one chance to seize a great opportunity!

KEEPING TRACK

Talk to others about how they have organized their information. Also, think about the times you have prepared big reports and projects for school. What has worked for you?

Keeping track of all the information you gather can be a big challenge. It's not as hard as it seems! You could mark file folders or large envelopes with the names of each college in which you are interested. Place any information you get in these files. Organize them alphabetically or by state, then keep them in a handy place. As you start narrowing your choices, you can keep the most important files in front and remove the others. You can also use your computer, a notebook, or index cards to keep track of additional information.

A chart can really help! Comparing colleges is more challenging than collecting information. Charts can help you bring a lot of information together in one place.

For example, make a list of all the criteria that matter to you most (overall size, availability of major, class size, competitiveness, and so forth). Next, rearrange the list in order of importance to you. Now you are ready to make a chart. Write your most important factors down one side of the chart. List the colleges you are considering across the top. Draw lines separating the rows and columns so that you have individual boxes. You can then mark in the boxes how each college rates for each characteristic. (See the example on the next page.) Leave room for short notes.

Your chart can be as general or specific as you would like. You can revise it as well, making it more specific or changing your priorities. Once your chart is complete, your planning work is done. You're now ready to apply to college!

Comparing Colleges

Criteria	College A	College B
4-year	4-year university	4-year college
Mid-Atlantic	Pennsylvania	Washington, D.C.
Rural/Suburban	yes	no
% Receiving Financial Aid	50%	65%
Student:Faculty	17:1	15:1
Majors Available		
—Performing Arts	yes	no
—Mathematics	yes	yes
—Physics	yes	yes
—Communications	no	yes
Requires B Average	yes	yes
Public Transportation Available	no	yes
Number of Undergraduates	1,900	4,300
Has Ice Hockey Team	yes	no
Annual Tuition	$14,500	$12,900

How Do I Apply to College?

You can apply to college by following basic steps in a straightforward, organized way. With your list of colleges in hand, you are ready to begin!

If you plan to attend college right after high school, you will complete your applications during your senior year. The amount of effort will depend on the number of places where you are applying and their selectivity. More selective colleges have more steps and requirements.

Being organized will make the process much easier. In this chapter, we will explain many of the steps involved in applying to college.

THE ADMISSIONS OFFICE

At some colleges, the admissions office has other names. These include the office of enrollment services, the office of entry services, and the office of records and registration.

The admissions office helps people learn about the college and works with students who are in the process of applying. It is also responsible for deciding who will be admitted.

The people who work in the admissions office—the dean, counselors, recruiters, and assistants—can provide you with application forms. They can answer your questions about the college, provide general materials such as viewbooks, help you set up interviews, and arrange campus tours, open houses, and other special programs.

 ## APPLICATION FORMS

Open admissions as well as selective and competitive colleges were discussed in Chapter 8.

Colleges require you to provide different amounts of information when you apply. Generally, those colleges that have open admissions require the least amount of information. Selective and competitive colleges tend to ask for more materials.

Application forms and procedures can change. Be sure you have current forms. Know the procedures for the year you are applying.

At its simplest, the application form is a one- or two-page form. This form asks basic questions about your name, address, telephone number, date of birth, race, ethnic background, and citizenship. This form may also ask questions about your high school background and college goals.

Activities outside of the classroom are often called extracurricular activities.

More selective colleges ask for more information. They will ask you about yourself, your school record, your interests and activities, and your goals in life. They may ask you to write essays and to provide standardized test scores, an evaluation from your high school, and recommendations from teachers and others.

A Picture of Who You Are

At the heart of every application are questions the college asks to learn more about you.

What personal information does a college want to know? In addition to basic information, many colleges ask you about your school background. They ask where you are currently attending school and where you have gone to school in the past. Many colleges will ask about your personal and academic goals.

Some colleges are interested in knowing about your family. They may ask what your parents do, whether they have attended college—and where—and whether any brothers or sisters have attended college. They may also ask about any places where you have lived or travelled.

Colleges are required by federal and state law to ask certain questions, such as race and ethnic background, gender, and citizenship. You may not be required to answer all these questions. However, any information you provide must be truthful and accurate!

Why do colleges ask these questions? Colleges have many reasons for asking these questions. In many cases, they are simply trying to get a better sense of the complete you! They are also trying to find out if you have the qualifications to be successful and happy at the college.

Many colleges want students with different backgrounds. Students learn not only from teachers and books, but also from each other.

Colleges may ask about your intended major. For example, if they accept only students who plan to major in biology, there may not be enough lab space to go around! By knowing more about you, colleges can plan for the kinds of services they will need to provide for you.

YOUR SCHOOL RECORD

Colleges often ask that your high school transcript be sent directly from your high school. The transcript is an official record of your courses and grades.

Your school record—grades, grade point average, courses, and class rank—is an important part of getting into college. You may be asked specific questions about your performance in school. In addition, many applications include a form to be completed by your high school's college advisor or guidance counselor.

Colleges with selective admissions will check to see if you meet their standards for being accepted. Colleges with competitive admissions are not only looking at your record, but also comparing it to records of other students who have applied.

Your grade point average is a number that summarizes your overall grades. An A is usually worth four points, a B three points, a C two points and a D one point. If your overall average is 3.3, you have the equivalent of a B+ average.

Grades and GPA (Grade Point Average). By themselves, neither your grades nor your grade point average gives a complete picture of your school performance. For example, they do not show how difficult your courses have been.

Colleges look for patterns. Have your grades been consistent from year to year? Have you shown an ongoing improvement or have your grades fallen over time? Are your grades consistent across your courses? Or are you strong in some subjects and weak in others?

Many schools use percentages instead of points or letter grades. For instance, 90% and higher may be equivalent to an A. Check with your guidance counselor to find out about the grading system at your school.

Suppose Terry earns all *C*s freshman year, all *B*s sophomore year, and all *A*s junior year. During the same time, Pat earns all *A*s freshman year, all *B*s sophomore year, and all *C*s junior year. Their overall grades and their grade point averages are the same. However, on this basis alone, Terry will be considered the stronger candidate. Why? Because Terry is showing ongoing improvement.

Your courses. Colleges look to see what courses you have taken. They are interested in seeing the level of difficulty of your courses and the types of courses you have chosen. For example, some students are stronger in math than other students. If you are planning to apply to an engineering college or a pre-med program, the college may want to see that you have made it at least as far as precalculus in your math classes.

One student may have straight As in average courses, while another has straight Bs in honors courses. The first student has higher grades, but the second student will probably be rated higher by colleges.

The same subjects are taught at different levels. Many high schools offer courses at an honors level. These courses are considered to be more challenging than other courses. Some high schools also offer Advanced Placement (AP) courses. If you successfully complete an advanced placement class, then you may take the AP exam. In turn, if you score well enough on the AP exam, you may be able to earn credit toward your college degree.

What is class rank? One way that secondary schools have to compare performance is to rank each student. A student who is ranked number 1 is considered to have the highest academic achievement of all the students in that grade.

If a senior class has 100 students, then the twenty students with the highest rank graduate in the top fifth of their class.

Many schools calculate class rank by using grade point averages. In this case, the student with the highest GPA is ranked first. However, some high schools use a ranking system that gives students more credit for taking challenging courses.

Specific class rank is less important than rank relative to others. Suppose Lou's class has 75 students whereas Reggie's has 500. Both have a class rank of 40. Lou's rank is not in the top half. Reggie's is in the top ten percent.

Some colleges require a certain GPA for you to get automatic admission. Competitive colleges accept only some students who apply. Check the college guides to find out the typical class rank or GPA of students these colleges accept.

Your high school and admissions. Colleges also look at the high school you have attended and how it compares to other schools in your area. They learn about the courses offered, the grading system, and the performance of students who have gone on to college. Therefore, if you have attended a more challenging school with a proven track record, your grades and class rank may be looked at more favorably.

 ## Essays

Many applications ask you to write essays. Some essays are very specific, others fairly general. You may even be able to choose from several options. Essays serve several purposes. They provide a way for the college to get to know more about you. They also provide a sample of your writing and communication skills. Some sample essay questions are listed below.

Sample Essay Questions

a. If you could go back and change one day in your life, what would you change and why?

b. Choose one issue of international, national, or local concern that is of special interest to you. Describe your position on the issue, any personal involvement you may have had with the issue, and how you would resolve it.

c. You have just completed your 300 page autobiography. Please submit page 217.

d. If you could be anyone from the past, present, or future, who would you be and why?

YOUR ACTIVITIES

Many colleges look for students who combine a strong academic record with a good range of activities. Some will accept a B student with lots of activities before an A student with no activities.

Colleges want to know more about you than just what you have done in the classroom. They also want to know about your achievements outside of the classroom.

School activities. Colleges depend on students to contribute to the college community. If students do not get involved in campus activities, then the quality of that college suffers. Therefore, colleges are interested in students who have a track record of being involved.

Extracurricular activities can help you get into selective and competitive colleges. They can even help you get scholarships. Most important, they're fun and fulfilling—and a great way to make friends.

You will have an opportunity to tell the college about ways you have participated in your school. Were you active in plays or choirs? Did you work on the school newspaper or yearbook? Did you participate in student government? Were you a member of any clubs?

Athletics. Students who participate in athletics develop important skills in both cooperation and competitiveness. They develop leadership skills. They also show their ability to balance the time demands of the classroom with the demands of their particular sport.

Work. Many colleges are interested in knowing about your work experiences. Students who have worked can show that they have maturity and take responsibility for their lives.

Community service. Colleges are increasingly interested in students who can show a proven commitment to their community through civic, church, and other volunteer activities.

RECOMMENDATIONS

Recommendations are also called evaluations and reviews. Colleges usually provide special forms for recommendations.

Many colleges want to know what others think about you. Therefore, you may need to provide recommendations from others. Colleges usually want recommendations to come from one or two of your high school teachers. You may be able to provide additional recommendations, perhaps from your minister, employer, or someone else who has known you for a while.

Carefully follow the college's guidelines. Give plenty of notice to people writing your recommendations. Be sure that they know and can meet your deadline. And always thank them for their time and effort.

People writing recommendations are asked about more than just your proven ability. They are asked about your maturity, character, creativity, leadership, and potential for personal growth. They are asked to compare your abilities and potential to that of others the reviewer has known. Many recommendations, though not all, are confidential. In these cases, you will not know what has been written unless the person shares it with you.

 # INTERVIEWS

Interviews also provide you with a chance to get to know the college better.

While not all colleges require interviews, many strongly recommend them. If you cannot get to campus, they may arrange for you to meet with alumni who live near you.

Interview Tips

1. Know the time and place.
2. Be on time.
3. Dress appropriately.
4. Give a firm handshake.
5. Use good posture.
6. Make eye contact.
7. Speak clearly.
8. Be yourself.
9. Have questions ready.
10. Express your interest.
11. Thank your interviewer.
12. Send a thank-you note.

Special Considerations

What do you do if the application does not give you the chance to let a college know information that you think is important? It's perfectly fine to add this information. Be sure, however, that you pick what is truly important *and* stay within the overall guidelines that the college provides.

What other kinds of materials can I submit? Students who are performers or studio artists may need to provide additional materials. In fact, if you apply to a college that specializes in the arts, you may be asked to include a sample of your work: a portfolio with sample drawings or photos of sculptures or other artworks you have created, a tape of you playing an instrument or singing, a recording of others performing a piece you have composed. If you are an actor or dancer, you may need to send a videotape of you in performance. (Some colleges may require you to audition.) Check with the college about the best way to send them your supplemental materials.

Other considerations. You may have had life experiences that are relevant to your overall record. Some experiences may explain a short-term change in your performance. Perhaps your grades suffered during a time when you were ill or facing serious family problems.

In other cases, you may have had to overcome obstacles, such as long-term physical challenges. Essays often provide you with the opportunity to discuss these experiences. Be willing to share them with the college. They help the college get a more complete picture of who you are.

College Entrance Exams

Our single most important words of advice about college entrance exams: Do NOT wait until your senior year *of high school to start thinking about them! Be prepared.*

Selective and competitive colleges often require you to send scores from college entrance exams. These are standardized tests similar to ones that you may have taken in elementary and middle school. The two major exams, the SAT and the ACT, are offered several times a year throughout the country. You may take practice versions as early as seventh or eighth grade. Most students take these exams in their junior or senior year.

You can practice for the exams in many ways: books, sample tests, software, special classes, and tutoring.

Some colleges require one or another test. Other colleges will accept either. While test scores are only one factor, they can be an important factor. Your guidance counselor will be able to give you good advice about preparing for the tests, when to take them, and test procedures.

Major College Entrance Exams

SAT I. Scholastic Aptitude Test I. Two major parts: verbal and math; most questions multiple-choice; some math questions require you to supply answer.

SAT II. Scholastic Aptitude Test II. Formerly called Achievement Tests; cover specific subjects such as biology, world history, and French; most important for competitive colleges.

ACT. American College Testing. Multiple-choice tests in four areas: English, mathematics, reading, and science reading.

PSAT/NMSQT. Preliminary SAT/National Merit Scholarship Qualifying Test. Gives SAT practice and chance to qualify for college funds.

TOEFL. Test of English as a Foreign Language. Required of foreign students at many colleges.

SAT II Subject Tests Offered 1995-1996

English

Writing
Literature

History and Social Studies

American History and Social Studies
World History

Mathematics

Mathematics Level I
Mathematics Level IC
Mathematics Level IIC (Calculator)

Languages

Chinese with Listening
French
French with Listening
German
German with Listening
Modern Hebrew
Italian
Japanese with Listening
Latin
Spanish
Spanish with Listening
English Language Proficiency

Sciences

Biology
Chemistry
Physics

The SAT II Subject Tests cover specific topics in depth. Many students take these tests toward the end of the school year in which they studied the particular subject. For example, if you take a chemistry course as a high school sophomore, then you may take the SAT II Test in chemistry toward the end of your sophomore year.

Other important tests are the Advanced Placement or AP Tests. These are given to students who have taken an AP course during the school year. If you score well on these tests, you may receive credit toward your college graduation requirements. AP courses are not available everywhere.

COMPLETING THE APPLICATION

You will want to give yourself plenty of time to prepare the application. Try to get copies long before they are due. Be sure, however, to use a current application. Forms and procedures might change from year to year.

If you plan to apply for financial aid—money to help you with college costs—you will need to submit additional forms. We discuss financial aid in Chapter 11.

A chart can help you keep track of application materials and deadlines. List the colleges where you are applying, the information you need to provide, due dates, fees, and mailing dates.

The application often provides the college's first look at you. Be neat, complete, and on time. (Of course, don't forget you still have homework, school activities, and other responsibilities!)

Do not decide where to apply based only on whether or not they accept the common form. Choose colleges that are right for you. Then, if they happen to accept the common form, you can consider using it when you apply.

Are there easier ways of applying to college?
Several private colleges accept an application, known as the Common Application, in place of their own form. You complete this form once and mail it to colleges participating in the program. You will still need to send information such as recommendations and test scores to each college. But you will not need to complete the personal information each time. Your guidance counselor can help you get a Common Application and a list of colleges that accept it.

Computer options are also available. Several companies offer computerized application forms. Some format the information for you. In other cases, you can even apply electronically, sending most of your application to the college through your computer. Some of these options may be available through your high school.

Who Accepts the Common Application?*

State	College or University*
Arkansas	Hendrix College
California	Occidental College
Colorado	Colorado College
Connecticut	Fairfield University
Florida	Stetson University
Georgia	Emory University
Illinois	Knox College
Indiana	Earlham College
Iowa	Coe College
Kentucky	Centre College
Louisiana	Tulane University
Maine	Bates College
Maryland	Johns Hopkins University
Massachusetts	Simmons College
Michigan	Kalamazoo College
Minnesota	St. Olaf College
Mississippi	Millsaps College
New Hampshire	Dartmouth College
New Jersey	Drew University
New York	Rochester Institute of Technology
North Carolina	Wake Forest University
Ohio	Case Western Reserve University
Oklahoma	University of Tulsa
Oregon	Willamette University
Pennsylvania	Franklin and Marshall College
Tennessee	University of the South
Texas	Texas Christian University
Vermont	Middlebury College
Virginia	Randolph-Macon Woman's College
Washington	University of Puget Sound
Wisconsin	Ripon College
District of Columbia	George Washington University

*This list represents a small group of the colleges accepting the Common Application.

WHEN SHOULD I APPLY?

Colleges have different timetables for when they accept students. Your deadline for applying to a particular college is determined by its timetable.

Check with either the college catalog or the admissions office to confirm deadlines.

Competitive colleges with limited space usually have very strict deadlines for applications. Some colleges have priority deadlines—students who apply by this deadline may have a better chance of being accepted. Open admissions colleges will usually accept applications up until the start of each term.

Complete and send your applications as early as possible. At many colleges, applying early may enable you to be accepted earlier. You may also move to the head of the line for campus housing, financial aid, and enrolling in classes.

Quinnipiac College in Connecticut considers applications on a rolling admissions basis. Students generally have until February 15 to submit their applications. But once a program is filled, no more students are accepted into that program. If you want to enter the physical therapy program, you probably should submit your application well before February 15.

On the one hand, Mankato State University in Minnesota is a selective college. If you meet certain requirements, you will be admitted. For admission to most programs, deadlines are fairly close to the start of each term. On the other hand, the nursing program is competitive, with limited spaces. The deadlines for applying are stricter than for other programs.

Types of Admissions

Regular Decision. Selective and competitive colleges have varying cut-off dates for applications (December through March). You are usually notified mid-March to mid-April.

Rolling Admissions. Applications considered in order of receipt. Space can run out. Students applying earlier have better chance of acceptance. Final cut-off dates vary. Look for priority deadlines.

Open Admissions. Applications accepted until classes begin. Students guaranteed admission with few requirements. Earlier application usually provides better access to special programs and class selection.

Early Decision. Special opportunity offered to students with clear first choice. Applications due earlier than for regular admissions, generally by November 15. You are notified earlier and may have inside track for being accepted. But you may be restricted from applying elsewhere. Entrance exams should be completed junior year or early senior year.

January/Mid-Year Admissions. Some students do not start college in fall after high school graduation. Admission for a later term has different deadlines. Be sure college allows enrollment for term other than fall.

Early Admissions. Allows students to attend college full time instead of senior year of high school. For excellent and mature students. Apply during your junior year of high school.

Waiting List. Colleges accept more students than they have spaces for. They keep waiting lists in case space opens up. You may be accepted later. While waiting, accept another offer to be sure of space somewhere.

Transfer Admissions. Special guidelines for students who have already taken classes at another college. Guidelines may differ based on where you have attended. Many two-year colleges have special arrangements with four-year colleges. Transfer admission also affected by how many courses you have already taken and at what level. (See later in chapter to find out more about transferring.)

COSTS OF APPLYING

Most colleges charge a fee when you apply. The fee covers the costs that the college has when it considers your application. Fees at competitive colleges can be higher than fees at other colleges because the time needed to evaluate applications is greater. Fees also tend to be higher at private colleges than at public colleges.

Fees also discourage students from applying to colleges carelessly. They add up when you apply to several colleges. Fees encourage you to apply only to colleges where you really want to go and have a reasonable chance of being accepted.

Sometimes students cannot afford the application fee. Most colleges will waive the fee (not require the student to pay) in the case of financial hardship. Your guidance counselor or principal can help you learn more about fee waiver programs or write a letter for you requesting a waiver.

Sample Application Fees

College or University	Fee	College or University	Fee
Athens State College (AL)	$30	Ohio State Univ. (OH)	$30
Boston College (MA)	$50	Pomona College (CA)	$50
Bowdoin College (ME)	$50	Purdue University (IN)	$30
Concordia College (MN)	$15	Saint Louis Univ. (MO)	$25
Duke University (NC)	$55	Shippensburg Univ. (PA)	$20
Howard University (DC)	$25	Univ. of Hartford (CT)	$35
Lansing Comm. Coll. (MI)	$10	Univ. of Vermont (VT)	$45
Marquette University (WI)	$30	Univ. of Washington (WA)	$35
Miami-Dade CC (FL)	$15	Univ. of Wisconsin (WI)	$28
Montana State Univ (MT)	$30	Valencia Comm. Coll. (FL)	$20
Montgomery Coll. (MD)	$25	Valparaiso Univ. (IN)	$30

YOU'RE IN. NOW WHAT?!?

Once the admissions office has decided whether to admit you, it will notify you by mail. In most cases you will be accepted or rejected. In some cases, you may be placed on a waiting list—if space opens up later, you may be admitted.

Making a decision. After you are notified, the ball is back in your court. First, you must make a decision. Where will you go? If you have been accepted at several places, you must choose one.

Before deciding, visit the colleges if you can. Talk to family, friends, teachers, and counselors. Carefully weigh what each college offers. *Now is the time to consider costs and what you can afford.* Finally, use your best judgment.

Colleges usually try to notify you about financial aid at or near the time they offer you admission. You will not be expected to respond to an offer of admission until you know about the financial support you will be receiving.

If a college does not offer you enough money, you can contact the admissions office and explain any special circumstances you may face. If the college wants you enough, they may come up with a better offer. The worst they can say is no!

May 1 is the National Candidates Reply Date, used by most colleges. Having one date gives students time to consider all their options.

Once you have decided, notify the colleges of your decision. *You must respond to a college's admissions offer by its deadline (usually May 1), or you will lose your place.* Also, inform the colleges you are not choosing so that they can offer your place to a student on their waiting lists.

Send the deposit. Most colleges require you to make a deposit when you accept their offer of admission. The deposit goes toward your first year's expenses. It is often nonrefundable. The deposit is your commitment to the college. *If you do not send the deposit by the deadline, you may lose your place.*

If you are on a waiting list, you may find out later that space has opened up. Now you have a new decision to make. Evaluate again where you want to go—the college that has just accepted you or the college where you have already mailed your deposit. (Even though you may not get your deposit back, you may actually come out ahead financially if the college which had you on its waiting list is less expensive!) In any case, make your decision in terms of which college offers you the best overall opportunity.

Now am I done? No. You may now have been accepted, responded, and paid your deposit. However, you must still successfully complete high school. If you do not, the college can withdraw its acceptance.

What if I'm rejected? Colleges with limited spaces often have many more applicants than spaces. Unfortunately, they cannot accept every qualified student who applies. While you might be very disappointed if you do not get into your favorite college, focus on the positive.

Concentrate on the colleges that have accepted you. Many students look back on what at first seemed like a disappointment as the beginning of a wonderful opportunity somewhere else.

TRANSFERRING

If you want to transfer, check with the college for any special forms, procedures, and deadlines you must follow to be admitted.

Transfer students begin studying at one college and then switch to another college. Students who want to transfer apply to the second college. The process is similar, but not quite identical.

Why would someone transfer? For many reasons. Money is a major one. Perhaps you cannot afford the college you are attending and want to switch to one that's less expensive. The reverse is also true. You might begin at a less expensive college, saving money so that you can afford to transfer to a more expensive one.

Students transfer all the time for many reasons. In fact, so many transfer that most colleges have counselors whose main job is to help students transfer to or from other colleges.

Grades and performance are another factor. You might find yourself in over your head and want to switch to a less challenging college. On the other hand, you may have been hesitant about college, but find you are doing better than you expected. You may decide to look for a greater challenge.

Sometimes students who want to change majors transfer colleges. For instance, you might take sociology and psychology courses and discover you are very interested in social work. You may decide to switch to a college with a program that specializes in social work.

You may transfer for many other reasons as well. Perhaps your family has moved and you want to be closer. Perhaps you started by going away to college and find that you're homesick. The most common reason that students transfer, however, is to continue their studies. Community college students frequently transfer to four-year colleges to continue their education.

CHANGING YOUR MIND

Can you change your mind about where you will go to college? Absolutely! You can even change your mind after you have accepted an offer of admission. Of course, in that case, you may face some costs. If you have already sent a deposit to the college, do not expect to have it returned. And if you are receiving special grants or loans (see Chapter 11) you may not be able to use them at another college.

Many colleges can provide a deferred admission. You are accepted, but can take a semester or year off before you begin in order to achieve other goals. Check with the admissions office about this option.

However, if you find that the choice you have made is not the best one, you can look into other options. These include accepting another college's offer, applying to other colleges, or taking some time to work first and evaluate your goals. You may want to take a leave of absence—in this case, you leave the college for a short time, with an option to return. These choices are available to you whether you are already in college or have not yet started.

Many colleges, especially community colleges, have formal agreements with other colleges to ensure that students can transfer from one college to the other. These agreements are often called articulation agreements.

Again, be aware of costs. You may lose money already paid to the college. If you transfer, you may not be able to transfer all your credits. If you have already gone to one college for two years, you may still have to attend the second college for more than another two years in order to earn your degree.

Any decision about changing your mind should be made as carefully as your first decision to go to college. As before, talk to others. Do not make your decision on impulse. Above all, establish clear goals for yourself, even if they are different from your original ones. Take charge of yourself!

10 HOW MUCH DOES COLLEGE COST?

It depends. College can cost a lot. But exactly how much depends on many factors. Remember, your education is an investment in yourself.

You might wonder if college is worth the money. The answer is YES! We know that people with college degrees earn much more than people without them. And many careers will not be available to you without a college education.

In this chapter we will look at the different types of college costs. We'll also look at some actual examples so that you can get an idea of just how much the costs are.

TUITION

The total cost of college can vary a lot. Private (or independent) colleges, for example, tend to cost more than public colleges. Four-year colleges tend to cost more per year than two-year colleges. One of the biggest factors is whether you are a full-time or part-time student. And whether you live at the college, at home, or on your own can affect your overall costs.

Public colleges receive support from state or local tax dollars. Private colleges receive relatively little. Therefore, tuition at public colleges is already supported in part by the public.

College costs include your tuition, fees, books and supplies, and room and board. In addition, you need to factor in expenses such as transportation and other living costs.

What is tuition? The part of your costs that pays directly for your education is the tuition. Most of your tuition helps pay for the college's faculty and staff. Your tuition also helps pay the general costs of running the college and providing certain services—costs such as books and other materials for the library, computers for student use, and advising and career counseling.

The Cooper Union for the Advancement of Science and Art does not charge tuition to its students. Cooper Union, a top college for art, architecture, and engineering students, was set up in 1859 by Peter Cooper, an inventor and industrialist who had little schooling. Cooper believed that education, especially for children of immigrants and the working class, should be "as free as water or air." Money that Cooper and others set aside through the years has been invested and covers student tuition costs, although students have other expenses.

At many colleges (especially private, competitive colleges), tuition is your single biggest cost. At other colleges (especially public two-year and four-year colleges), tuition is less of a factor.

New buildings on campus are paid for by special funds, not by tuition. Special contributions also pay for equipment such as an electron microscope for the science department or new pianos for the music department.

No matter how much tuition costs, it does not cover all the costs of your college education. Taxes provide a lot of funding for public colleges and some funding for private ones. Contributions from alumni and other donors, grants from businesses and organizations, and earnings from a college's investments also help pay costs. Government grants that pay for faculty research are also very important to many colleges.

Students do not always pay full tuition. As we will see in Chapter 11, many receive some form of assistance paying for college.

California's public colleges and universities do not formally charge tuition to students who are residents of California. However, students are still responsible for college fees (which can equal tuition in other states) and living expenses. Students who are not residents of California pay an additional tuition fee. The amount they pay depends on whether they are attending a university, a college, or a community college. Among California's many public colleges are the University of California (e.g., the University of California, Berkeley and the University of California, Santa Barbara), California State University (e.g., Humboldt State University and San Jose State University) and numerous two-year colleges (e.g., American River College, Bakersfield College, College of the Redwoods, Los Angeles Pierce College, and Moorpark College).

Examples of Tuition at Four-Year Colleges

State	College or University	Full-Year Tuition
Alabama	Auburn University	+* $2,100
Alaska	University of Alaska—Anchorage	* 1,742
Arizona	University of Arizona	* $1,884
Arkansas	Henderson State University	* $1,728
California	University of the Pacific	$17,220
Colorado	Colorado School of Mines	* $4,284
Connecticut	University of Hartford	$14,220
Delaware	University of Delaware	* $3,860
Florida	Rollins College	$17,495
Georgia	Agnes Scott College	$13,800
Hawaii	University of Hawaii—Manoa	* $1,460
Idaho	Idaho State University	* $1,820
Illinois	DePaul University	$11,856
Indiana	Indiana University	* $2,984
Iowa	University of Northern Iowa	* $2,291
Kansas	Kansas State University	* $1,766
Kentucky	University of Louisville	* $2,170
Louisiana	Grambling State University	* $2,088
Maine	Maine Maritime Academy	* $3,880
Maryland	St. John's College	$18,630
Massachusetts	Boston University	$19,420
Michigan	University of Michigan	+* $5,040
Minnesota	Concordia College	$10,815
Mississippi	Alcorn State University	* $2,376
Missouri	Saint Louis University	$12,800
Montana	Rocky Mountain College	$9,610

In most cases, the tuition listed does not include student fees.
Tuition listed is for 1995-1996 year for full-time students.

*College is a public college. Tuition listed is for in-state residents.
  Students from out of state have higher costs.

+Tuition listed is for most programs at the university. Some programs, however, have a different tuition.

Examples of Tuition at Four-Year Colleges

State	College or University	Full-Year Tuition
Nebraska	Creighton University	$11,160
Nevada	Sierra Nevada College	$9,000
New Hampshire	Keene State College	*$2,740
New Jersey	Rutgers	* $3,640
New Mexico	University of New Mexico	* $1,997
New York	Polytechnic University	$15,300
North Carolina	East Carolina University	* $788
North Dakota	Minot State University	* $1,780
Ohio	Oberlin College	$20,600
Oklahoma	University of Tulsa	$11,750
Oregon	Reed College	$20,610
Pennsylvania	Villanova University	+$16,300
Rhode Island	Providence College	$14,400
South Carolina	Furman University	$13,440
South Dakota	Northern State University	* $1,508
Tennessee	Middle Tennessee State University	$1,616
Texas	Texas Tech University	* $840
Utah	Weber State University	* $1,377
Vermont	University of Vermont	* $6,468
Virginia	Virginia Military Institute	* $3,655
Washington	University of Puget Sound	$16,230
West Virginia	West Virginia Wesleyan College	$14,200
Wisconsin	Marquette University	+$13,010
Wyoming	University of Wyoming	* $1,686
District of Columbia	Trinity College	$11,750

In most cases, the tuition listed does not include student fees.
Tuition listed is for 1995-1996 year for full-time students.

*College is a public college. Tuition listed is for in-state residents.
 Students from out of state have higher costs.

+Tuition listed is for most programs at the university. Some programs, however, have a different tuition.

Examples of Tuition at Two-Year Colleges

State	College	Full-Year Tuition*
Alabama	Jefferson State Community College	$1,200
Alaska	Kenai Peninsula College	$1,794
Arizona	Yavapai College	$666
Arkansas	Garland County Community College	+ $792
California	Napa Valley College	$0
Colorado	Community College of Denver	$1,567
Connecticut	Housatonic Community Tech. College	$1,488
Delaware	Delaware Tech. & Community College	$1,200
Florida	Brevard Community College	$1,120
Georgia	Brunswick College	$1,074
Hawaii	Honolulu Community College	$504
Idaho	North Idaho College	$980
Illinois	Moraine Valley Community College	+ $1,320
Indiana	Indiana Vocational Technical College	$1,809
Iowa	Kirkwood Community College	$1,590
Kansas	Cloud County Community College	$810
Kentucky	Paducah Community College	$984
Louisiana	Bossier Parish Community College	+ $640
Maine	Southern Maine Technical College	$1,392
Maryland	Howard Community College	+ $2,130
Massachusetts	Bunker Hill Community College	$2,250
Michigan	Grand Rapids Community College	+ $1,581
Minnesota	Rainy River Community College	$2,004
Mississippi	Hinds Community College	$1,020
Missouri	Jefferson College	+ $1,240
Montana	Dawson Community College	+ $840

In most cases, the tuition listed does not include student fees. Tuition listed is for 1995-1996 year for full-time students.

*College is a public college. Tuition listed is for in-state residents. Students from out of state have higher costs.

+Indicates that the cost is for area residents. In-state and out-of-state residents have higher costs.

Examples of Tuition at Two-Year Colleges

State	College or University	Full-Year Tuition*
Nebraska	Mid-Plains Community College	$900
Nevada	Truckee Meadows Community College	$1,005
New Hampshire	New Hampshire Technical Institute	$2,304
New Jersey	Brookdale Community College	+ $1,860
New Mexico	New Mexico Junior College	+ $456
New York	Genesee Community College	$1,950
North Carolina	Blue Ridge Community College	$557
North Dakota	Bismarck State College	$1,552
Ohio	Columbus State Community College	$1,980
Oklahoma	Oklahoma City Community College	$780
Oregon	Mt. Hood Community College	$1,440
Pennsylvania	Community College of Philadelphia	+ $1,980
Rhode Island	Community College of Rhode Island	$1,566
South Carolina	Spartanburg Technical College	+ $850
South Dakota	Lake Area Vocational Technical Institute	$1,800
Tennessee	Shelby State Community College	$966
Texas	Tomball College	$713
Utah	Salt Lake Community College	$1,194
Vermont	Community College of Vermont	$1,365
Virginia	Rappahannock Community College	$1,493
Washington	Big Bend Community College	$1,296
West Virginia	Southern West Virginia Comm. College	$1,030
Wisconsin	Western Wisconsin Technical College	$1,535
Wyoming	Laramie County Community College	$760

*In most cases, the tuition listed does not include student fees.
Tuition listed is for 1995-1996 year for full-time students.*

**College is a public college. Tuition listed is for in-state residents.
Students from out of state have higher costs.*

*+Indicates that the cost is for area residents. In-state and out-of-state residents have
higher costs.*

Is tuition more if I attend a college outside of my home state?   Most private colleges charge all students the same amount of tuition no matter where they live. Most public colleges charge a higher tuition to students from other states. Keep in mind that public colleges are supported by tax dollars. The state's residents are already helping to pay for the college. Students who are residents of that state benefit from the taxes paid.

The good news is that you don't have to live in a particular state to attend its public colleges. Fewer spots may be available for out-of-state students. And you may have to pay a higher tuition. But if you are a good student, you may be accepted to a public college in another state.

At Elgin Community College in Illinois, the 1995-1996 tuition for full-time area residents was $1,185. For state residents outside the local area, full-time tuition was $3,840. Students from other states paid $4,712.

Many community colleges have three levels of tuition. Students from the county or nearby area pay the lowest tuition. Students from the state, but outside the local area, pay a state tuition. Students from outside the state pay the most.

In states such as North Carolina, all community colleges charge the same tuition. You pay the same tuition at one community college as you do at another. Other expenses may vary.

In some states, arrangements allow students from neighboring states to pay the resident tuition rate at public colleges. For example, Minnesota students at South Dakota State University pay the same tuition as South Dakota residents. Also, students from states in the Western Undergraduate Exchange (WUE) pay more than South Dakota residents but less than students from other states.

Residency Makes a Difference!

College or University	Resident Tuition*	Nonresident Tuition*
Albany State College (GA)	$1,840	$5,520
Appalachian State Univ. (NC)	$800	$7,600
Austin Peay State University (TN)	$1,878	$5,812
Bluefield State College (WV)	$1,856	$4,498
Boise State University (ID)	$0	$4,186
Buffalo State College (NY)	$2,650	$6,250
Fort Hays State University (KS)	$1,902	$6,169
Frostburg State University (MD)	$3,072	$6,548
Humboldt State University (CA)	$0	$7,380
Murray State University (KY)	$1,680	$5,040
Northern Michigan University	$2,900	$5,200
Oregon State University	$3,048	$9,096
Rhode Island College	$2,477	$6,995
Shippensburg University (PA)	$3,086	$7,844
Southeastern Louisiana University	$1,910	$3,998
Southern Connecticut State Univ.	$3,128	$8,820
Texas Tech University	$900	$5,280
University of Akron (OH)	$3,192	$7,954
University of Central Arkansas	$1,538	$3,362
University of North Dakota	$2,428	$5,952
University of North Florida	$1,820	$6,390
University of South Alabama	$2,352	$3,402
University of Southern Colorado	$1,683	$7,384
Univ. of Wisconsin—Stevens Pt.	$2,395	$7,422
University of Wyoming	$2,005	$6,403
Virginia Commonwealth Univ.	$3,034	$10,217
Western New Mexico University	$1,454	$5,308
Western Washington University	$2,406	$8,124
William Paterson College of NJ	$3,072	$4,064
Winthrop University (SC)	$3,801	$6,601

In most cases, the tuition listed does not include student fees. Tuition listed for these four-year public colleges is for 1995-1996 year for full-time students.

FEES

In addition to tuition, colleges charge students fees. Most fees are for very specific purposes. The amount may vary depending on your major or courses, the number of classes you take, and where you live, as well as other reasons.

The general fee may also be called a university fee or a consolidated fee.

Why do colleges charge general fees? Most colleges charge all students a general fee. This fee covers administrative costs—for example, the cost for the college to maintain its records of you. This fee may cover insurance, including health services that provides you with medical care while you are at the college.

At many colleges, the general fee and the student activity fee are combined into one. In fact, each college sets up its own combination of the fees.

What other types of fees do colleges charge? Some fees are very specific. Student activity fees help pay for student government, organizations, and publications on campus. Many colleges give the student government one big block of money to divide among the different clubs and groups. The student leaders then set priorities and decide how much money each group receives. This fee may also cover your use of the athletic and other facilities on campus.

Colleges may also charge students fees if they are late registering for classes (Chapter 12) or for many other specific reasons.

Students who commute or keep a car on campus usually pay parking fees. Class and lab fees help pay the costs of equipment, supplies, activities, and special insurance. Transaction fees—found at some colleges—are charges students pay to register each term, to drop or add a class after the registration period ends, or to get a copy of their grades (transcript). These fees are paid only by students who use the service. Many colleges charge a graduation fee to pay for your diploma.

Some Fees at the University of Miami (FL) 1995-1996

University Fee	included in tuition*
Student Activity Fee	(per semester) $70.25
Athletic Fee	(per semester) $24.50
Wellness Center Fee	(per semester) $85.00
Diploma Fee	no charge for original
Transcript Fee	$5.00
Clinical Nursing Student Insurance (liability)	(per year) $100.00
Readmission Fee	$ 20.00
Late Registration Fee	$100.00 and up
Parking	(per year) $115.00
Music Lessons (for non-music majors)	(per semester) $100.00

*University fee included in tuition for full-time undergraduates. Part-time and other students (e.g., graduate) pay separate fee per semester.

 ## BOOKS AND SUPPLIES

Most students are not used to buying books for their classes until they get to college. For most classes, you will need to purchase one or more textbooks. You may also need to buy study guides, lab manuals, solutions manuals, software, tapes, and CDs. Book prices vary considerably from $5 to $10 for small paperbacks to as much as $100 for upper level courses.

You will need to purchase other supplies. You may need a graphing calculator or software for some classes, lab kits, art supplies, and so forth. Most colleges estimate costs for books and supplies to be between $200 and $500 per term.

Some colleges also require you to buy a computer. Others simply recommend one. Colleges usually offer computers at reasonable prices.

Room and Board

Living arrangements are discussed in Chapter 13.

Living expenses are a major cost of college for many students, especially for those who live on campus. The cost of having somewhere to live is called room and the cost of meals is called board.

Even if you don't plan to live on campus, you still have to estimate room and board costs. You may live in an apartment of your own or with friends—your rent would be equivalent to room. And whether you eat on campus or off, you still need to budget a certain amount for meals or board.

Many colleges require their freshmen to live on campus. Colleges with on-campus housing will list the amount of room and board in their catalog along with tuition and fees.

Meal programs vary from college to college. In many cases, you can choose different programs. You may pay a flat fee that covers all your meals for the term. You may also choose programs that pay for a certain number of meals or charge you meal by meal.

Sample Annual Room and Board Costs*

Berklee College of Music (MA)	$7,190	Ripon College (WI)	$4,100
Dartmouth College (NH)	$6,069	Seattle University (WA)	$4,890
Ellsworth Comm. College (IA)	$2,920	Stephens College (MO)	$5,200
Emporia State University (KS)	$3,145	Tyler Junior College (TX)	$2,100
Fisk University (TN)	$3,690	University of Idaho	$3,600
Jacksonville University (FL)	$4,580	University of New Mexico	$2,916
Kenyon College (OH)	$3,690	Ursinus College (PA)	$5,160
Pacific University (OR)	$4,100	Valparaiso University (IN)	$3,450
Paul Smith's College (NY)	$4,230	Yuba College (CA)	$3,400

Costs vary year to year and are based on the type of housing and meal plan chosen.

Other Costs

You will also need to plan for several other costs. One major cost is transportation. If you commute to campus each day, you may have to pay for gas, tolls, and maintenance for your car, or for public transportation. If you live on campus without a car, you still need to think about the cost of getting to and from college at the start and end of the year. You should also estimate the cost of any travel you have during the year, whether for school vacations, holidays, or other trips.

Many colleges offer laundry plans for students living on campus. The plans may cover only sheets and towels or other laundry as well.

You also will need to consider living expenses. Basic supplies such as clothing, toothpaste, and school supplies need to be budgeted. The same is true for laundry. While many events on campus are free to students, others cost money. Concerts, going out to eat, some sporting events, and other events all cost money.

See the next page for a sample chart on college costs.

Your best bet is to make a chart in which you write down all of your expenses. In fact, you may need to make several charts, one for each college where you plan to apply. Not only will tuition, fees, and room and board costs vary; so too will these other costs. (For example, your transportation costs for going to a college away from home will be different than for a nearby college.)

Do not be too conservative when thinking about costs. You are better off planning for higher expenses and having money left over than finding that you do not have enough resources to cover your costs. When you have estimated the costs, you can start figuring out how to pay them, as we will see in the next chapter.

Estimating College Costs

College Name: _____

Tuition: $_____

Fees: University/General $_____
        Activity $_____
        Athletic $_____
        Lab $_____
        Courses (e.g., music) $_____
        Parking $_____
        Other Fees $_____
        TOTAL OF FEES $_____

Books and Supplies: $_____

Room and Board $_____
        Snacks/Other Meals $_____
        TOTAL FOR ROOM AND BOARD $_____

Transportation:
        Local and Long Distance $_____

Living Expenses:
        Clothing and Laundry $_____
        Personal Supplies $_____
        Entertainment $_____
        Telephone $_____
        Miscellaneous $_____
        TOTAL FOR LIVING EXPENSES $_____

Other Expenses: (e.g., tutoring) $_____

TOTAL ESTIMATED COSTS: $_____

11 HOW WILL I PAY FOR COLLEGE?

You can pay for college in more ways than you may expect! Figuring out how much college costs is only one step. Another important step is figuring out how much you can afford to pay. The trick is finding the money to pay the difference between the amount you have and the amount you need.

You're not alone in trying to find money to pay for college. Colleges themselves work very hard to provide as much support as possible for their students. You can draw on other sources as well, especially the government. With some good planning, some hard work, and, yes, a bit of luck, you can afford to go to a wide variety of colleges!

WAYS TO PAY

The different ways you can pay for college fall into four categories: family savings and income, grants and scholarships, loans, and work. Most students pay for college using some combination of these financial resources.

The money to pay for college may come from both you and your family. Some parents are able to set up a college savings fund for their kids. Your parents' salaries may be enough to pay for your college costs, depending on the college.

 Grants and scholarships provide money that you usually do not need to repay. You may need to make a certain commitment in order to receive this funding. For instance, programs like ROTC cover some of your expenses in exchange for taking on a military service commitment.

Loans are funds that you borrow from others. You are expected to pay back the loans over a period of time. Some loans must be repaid quickly, but others can be repaid over many years.

Another way to help pay for college is by working your way through college. Whether you go to college full-time or part-time while working will depend on how much money you need, the kind of student you are, and the kind of job you have.

Many colleges have work-study programs that provide students with jobs on campus. Such programs either pay you a wage for your work or allow you to work in exchange for tuition and other expenses.

WHAT IS FINANCIAL AID?

The majority of students need some sort of help paying for college. Every college has a financial aid office that works with students to try to give them that help. The different kinds of support that you can receive—grants, scholarships, loans, and work-study—are all part of financial aid.

Some state governments have college funds that are available through state politicians. For example, state senators may be able to award grants to students from their legislative district.

Where does financial aid come from? Support comes from many different sources. The federal government is one of the most important sources. For many years, the federal government has provided a wide range of support to students. State governments also provide support. Each state has its own programs for helping students.

Corporations are an important source of aid. They are interested in seeing that students are well educated for entering the work force. Corporations help in several ways. Some give money directly to the colleges. Others provide support directly to students. Many corporations have programs that support the children of their employees. And many match the donations that their employees make to colleges.

Colleges themselves are a major source of aid to students. Most set aside part of their annual budget to provide support. Colleges often run special fundraising programs aimed at providing financial aid.

Special organizations called foundations are also important sources of aid. Foundations give money to special causes such as medical research and care, the arts, environmental protection, and help for the homeless. Educational support is among their top priorities.

Other sources of aid are churches and synagogues, service organizations such as the Rotary Club and the Kiwanis, and wealthy individuals.

How do I qualify for financial aid?   You can qualify for most financial aid in several ways, including need, merit, and affiliation.

Most aid is need-based and is given to students who do not have the financial resources to pay for college. This kind of aid is available not only to students, but also to parents to help pay tuition.

Each year, thousands of students across the country receive National Merit Scholarships. Your qualification for these scholarships is based on your scores from the PSAT test taken in high school (see Chapter 9).

Merit-based aid goes to students who are successful in academics or other areas. For example, top academic students may receive merit-based aid.

You probably have heard about top athletes who receive aid when they play for a college. You can also get merit-based aid if you have special musical, artistic, or dramatic talent. You can receive aid by serving your community, organizing food drives, raising money for charity, and so forth.

Affiliation-based aid goes to students who meet criteria such as race, religion, and gender. For example, the United Negro College Fund provides support for African-American college students. Many religious groups provide support both at the national and local levels.

Some programs provide support for either male or female students. Every year, the Miss America Pageant provides millions of dollars of financial support to thousands of female students.

Where you live can also be a factor. Some aid is given to students from a certain geographical area. Still other aid is based on your future career. For example, some aid goes to students planning to become teachers in states where shortages exist.

Your EFC is subtracted from your estimated college costs (including room and board) to determine your financial need. Suppose your EFC is $5,000. If your estimated college costs are $4,000, then you have no need, according to the formula. If your estimated costs are $20,000, then you would have a need of $15,000.

How is need calculated? Need is the difference between a college's costs and what you and your family can afford to pay. Congress uses a formula to figure out your expected family contribution, or EFC, the amount of your family's resources Congress calculates should go toward college.

The EFC formula may not always seem fair. However, all families are measured the same way.

Important factors include family income, benefits such as social security payments, and assets such as savings and checking accounts, savings bonds, and investments (e.g., mutual funds and stocks).

When you repay a loan, you often send a payment every month for several years.

How do loan programs work? You may be able to borrow money for college from many sources, including the government, colleges, and banks. Loans are also available to parents. In a typical loan, you borrow a sum of money for a certain period of time. In addition to repaying the money, you pay interest charges. In some cases, you may also need to pay origination fees—fees that may be charged when you first apply for the loan.

Some loans are given to students who show need. Others (often with higher interest rates) are available regardless of need.

Many educational loans charge lower interest rates than loans for other purposes, such as buying a car or taking a vacation. And some college loans have lower interest rates than others. Loans with the lowest rates are often given to students who have the greatest financial need.

Many loans are deferred loans—you don't have to make any payments until you graduate. In many of these cases, no interest is charged while you are in college. Some loans can also be deferred for a short while to give you time to find work.

What are grants and scholarships? While you have to repay loans, you do not have to repay grants and scholarships.

In addition to the Pell Grants, supplemental grants may be available to students who have exceptional needs. As with all grants, you should speak with your guidance counselor for more information.

Pell Grants, available from the federal government, are awarded to a limited number of undergraduates who have the greatest need. In the 1995-96 school year, they provided up to $2,340 for the year. Not all students get the full award. Many states also provide grants to students.

Several national organizations provide scholarships to students, often on the basis of merit. We've already mentioned National Merit Scholarships, which are awarded to several thousand students every year. Major corporations also provide aid. For example, the Coca-Cola Company sponsors a scholarship program that is like the National Merit Scholarships in many ways. Its program has ties to the ACT entrance exam.

You can also win monetary prizes and awards based on your college performance. While some of these are small amounts of money, they do provide additional aid.

Colleges themselves are a major source of aid, both need-based and merit-based. Companies and individuals set up various scholarship programs for students at specific colleges. Many scholarships are for one year only, though some can be renewed. Be sure you know the terms of any scholarships you are offered.

The University of Tennessee, Knoxville, has more than a thousand scholarships available to its students. These funds are in addition to grants and loans available from the federal or state government. The 1995-96 catalog lists most of these scholarships, many of which are privately funded. The university's colleges and schools also provide awards to gifted students.

Sometimes you must fulfill a requirement to get a scholarship—otherwise you repay the money. For example, you may need to maintain a certain grade point average or major in a particular subject.

Most colleges have scholarships that have been set up to honor someone. In many cases, people set up a fund in memory of a relative or friend. When the fund reaches a certain level, it becomes an endowment. The money is then invested and any earnings from the endowment are used to provide scholarships. In this way, the relatives and friends have created a lasting memory, and one which helps students for years to come.

Some Scholarships at Wesleyan University (CT)

Chase. Given to a freshman from southern California, preferably one whose parents did not attend college; established in honor of a graduate.

Class of 1937. Given to students at start of their senior year, based on academics, citizenship, and community service.

Class of 1989. Provides financial support for freshman year to Native American, Chicano, or other underrepresented ethnic group.

Emily White Pendleton. Given primarily to dance majors.

Gram. Given to economics majors; established by a graduate.

Heim-Van Etten. Given to students in history, mathematics, or physical science based on character and seriousness of purpose.

Ray. Given to an Asian-American or African-American freshman in honor of Wesleyan's first minority student; may be renewed.

Regional. About fifteen four-year awards given to students coming to Wesleyan from far away.

Schumann. Awarded to freshmen who are from New Jersey, preferably to minority or disadvantaged students from Essex County.

Spada. Given to a freshman from a Hartford (CT) public high school; established by a graduate to honor his parents.

Many on-campus jobs (sorting mail, serving meals, shelving books, answering phones, providing campus tours, etc.) go to students who are in work-study programs. The college may limit the number of hours that students work each week. Many campus jobs are available to students with need, but may also be available to other students.

How are work-study programs set up? Work-study programs give aid to students by providing them with jobs during the school year. While many of the jobs are on campus, some are with public agencies or nonprofit organizations off campus. Many work-study programs are federally funded; others are funded by individual states or colleges.

In some cases, a work-study job may match a student's major. An art major might be able to get a job with either an on-campus or local museum. A student majoring in biology might be able to get a job in an on-campus research lab or with a biotechnology company in the area.

What aid is available from the military? If you enter a branch of the military, you will be eligible for various benefits that help you pay for college during and after your service.

Students who apply to military academies must be nominated. Most nominations come from members of Congress, though there are other ways to be nominated.

Students who attend military academies such as the United States Air Force Academy do not pay tuition. In fact, they receive monthly pay to cover their costs. Many colleges offer Reserved Officer Training Corps (ROTC) programs affiliated with a specific branch of the military. Students enrolled in these programs may get full scholarships or monthly allowances to go toward their education.

*Students who receive loans have a respon-sibility to repay their loans. **Do not accept aid *unless you fully understand and accept those respon-sibilities.****

What is a financial aid package? The financial aid office tries to develop the best combination of grants, loans, and work-study it can to match your needs. This combination is your financial aid package. Two students might receive the same total amount, but different packages. One student's support may be mostly grants, while a second student's is mostly loans and work-study.

A Financial Aid Sampler: The University of Louisville (KY) 1994-95

FEDERAL AND STATE PROGRAMS

Federal Pell Grant. For students with great need.

Federal Supplemental Education Opportunity Grant (SEOG). For students with exceptional need.

Federal Work-Study Program. Campus and community service jobs.

Federal Perkins Loan. Low interest loans through the college.

Federal Stafford Loan Program. Low-interest loans.

Parent's Loan for Undergraduate Students (PLUS). Low-cost loans.

Kentucky State Grant Program. For Kentucky residents.

SCHOLARSHIP PROGRAMS

Trustees' Scholarships. Five categories for Kentucky residents:

• National Merit Semifinalists and National Achievement Semifinalists.

• Governor's Scholars Award.

• Eagle Scout (Boy Scouts) Awards and Gold (Girl Scouts) Awards.

• Woodford R. Porter, Sr. Scholarships. Awarded to African-American students with strong academic record.

• The Dr. Martin Luther King, Jr. Endowment of Peace Award. Provides all-expenses-paid scholarships based on academic and leadership record.

Commonwealth and President's Scholarship Programs.

Community College Transfer Scholarship Program.

New Adult Learners Scholarship Program. For Kentucky residents who are 22 years of age and older who are new or returning to college.

Adult Learners Scholarship Program. For continuing students who are 22 years of age and older with proven academic record.

PRIVATELY FUNDED SCHOLARSHIPS/OTHER PROGRAMS.

Short-Term Tuition Loans.

Emergency Loan Funds. Small short-term loans.

Kentuckiana Regional Awards. Engineering and music students from selected counties.

Senior Citizens Program. Free tuition for older Kentucky residents.

Veteran's Educational Benefits.

Vocational Rehabilitation Assistance. For disabled students.

Tuition Waiver Programs. For Dependents of Deceased or Disabled Kentucky Veterans, Law Officers, and Firefighters.

Financial Aid at Four-Year Colleges

State	College or University	Percentage of Freshmen Who Receive Aid
Alabama	Samford University	80%
Alaska	Alaska Pacific University	93%
Arizona	Northern Arizona University	60%
Arkansas	University of the Ozarks	63%
California	Occidental College	78%
Colorado	University of Northern Colorado	74%
Connecticut	Fairfield University	69%
Delaware	Delaware State College	74%
Florida	Florida International University	38%
Georgia	Oglethorpe University	90%
Hawaii	Hawaii Pacific University	39%
Idaho	University of Idaho	65%
Illinois	Knox College	92%
Indiana	University of Evansville	96%
Iowa	University of Iowa	65%
Kansas	Wichita State University	24%
Kentucky	Cumberland College	90%
Louisiana	Louisiana Tech University	77%
Maine	Bates College	52%
Maryland	Western Maryland College	85%
Massachusetts	Merrimack College	82%
Michigan	Northern Michigan University	69%
Minnesota	Bemidji State University	78%
Mississippi	Delta State University	62%
Missouri	Webster University	82%
Montana	Rocky Mountain College	85%

A large percentage of community college students receive financial aid. For example, well over half the freshmen attending El Paso Community College in Texas receive some combination of grants, loans, and work.

Financial Aid at Four-Year Colleges

State	College or University	Percent of Freshmen Who Receive Aid
Nebraska	Creighton University	86%
Nevada	University of Nevada—Las Vegas	50%
New Hampshire	Franklin Pierce College	76%
New Jersey	Stevens Institute of Technology	75%
New Mexico	New Mexico Highlands University	80%
New York	Fordham University	90%
North Carolina	Appalachian State University	44%
North Dakota	Dickison State University	75%
Ohio	University of Dayton	96%
Oklahoma	University of Tulsa	76%
Oregon	Lewis & Clark College	70%
Pennsylvania	Slippery Rock University	80%
Rhode Island	Salve Regina University	78%
South Carolina	Clemson University	59%
South Dakota	Black Hills State University	70%
Tennessee	Vanderbilt University	55%
Texas	Rice University	80%
Utah	Southern Utah University	68%
Vermont	Johnson State College	67%
Virginia	George Mason University	48%
Washington	Western Washington University	65%
West Virginia	Marshall University	55%
Wisconsin	Ripon College	82%
Wyoming	University of Wyoming	58%
District of Columbia	Catholic University	76%

Some financial aid is restricted to freshmen. However, many scholarships and grants are set aside for juniors and seniors who have declared their majors and who have a track record of success in college.

PAYMENT PLANS

Most colleges send bills for tuition, fees, and any room and board in advance of each term. Many colleges also offer plans that allow you to spread out the payments during the school year.

For instance, Rollins College in Florida expects payment for its fall term by late July and payment for its spring term by late December. It also offers a ten-month payment plan—you pay equal amounts each month starting in June.

Some Perkins loans may be forgiven (you don't need to repay all or part). For example, full-time special education teachers, math and science teachers in areas with few teachers, and Peace Corps volunteers may not have to pay back all of the loan.

Many loan programs offer several repayment plans. Choices may change from year to year. You will want to talk with your financial aid officer before taking on any loans in order to make sure you understand all your available options.

In some cases, loans can be deferred (you can delay when the payments begin). For instance, if you go on to graduate school or are unable to find work, payments may be deferred.

Federal Loan Repayment Plans

Income Contingent Repayment Plan. Your monthly payment based on annual income and loan amount; you have up to 25 years to repay.

Extended Repayment Plan. Allows repayment over 12 to 30 years; lower monthly payment than standard plan, but higher interest costs.

Graduated Repayment Plan. Loans repaid in 12 to 30 years; early payments are low; monthly amount increases every two years.

Standard Repayment Plan. Fixed amount due monthly for 10 years.

OTHER WAYS TO PAY

As you look for ways to pay for college, you may be surprised at what's available, especially in your own community. While you have to put in extra work to find this support, the results can be well worth the effort. And even though these other grants and scholarships may be smaller, they can really add up!

Churches and synagogues often provide small grants to members of their congregation who are going on to college. Many service and business organizations based in the community like to award scholarships to students who have a good track record of community service.

Large companies often support students from the area. In many cases, support is geared especially to students whose parents work for the company. And smaller companies also may provide support. You can always ask the owner or manager of a local business if they provide any grants. Even if they don't, you may be able to persuade them to start! If they offer a grant that is announced at your high school awards ceremonies, the business has received some good advertising while doing a good deed! You may only get $50 or $100, but every bit helps!

Students who receive aid, especially grants and scholarships, often make donations to the college after they graduate. Their support helps the next generation of students to pay for college, just as the previous generation helped them.

Thousands of scholarships are available and they are given for all sorts of reasons. But did you know that thousands of them go unawarded each year because students don't apply for them? The worst that can happen if you apply is that you won't be chosen. However, if you don't apply, the one thing you can be sure of is that you won't be chosen!

APPLYING FOR FINANCIAL AID

Applying for financial aid starts with gathering information.

Ask your counselor about getting a copy of The Student Guide: Financial Aid *from the U.S. Department of Education. This booklet is free to students. You can also write to the* Federal Student Aid Information Center, P.O. Box 84, Washington, D.C. 20044-0084.

How can I gather information? Contact three important resources: your school guidance office, reference librarians, and financial aid offices. Counselors can give you an overview and details about important changes and deadlines, especially with federal financial aid. They can provide information packets, including forms you will need. Some guidance offices offer both financial aid workshops and computerized search services.

Reference librarians can show you books written specifically about paying for college. They can lead you to information about foundations that give grants to students.

Financial aid offices can tell you about aid that is available specifically at their college. Most federal aid availability is the same from college to college. But state, local, and private aid vary.

But don't stop there! Attend college fairs. Have your parents check the personnel offices where they work about other benefits. Many grants are given to people who meet special criteria. You might be one of those people! Don't wait for financial aid to come to you. Take an active role!

Like many other colleges, Hofstra University in New York publishes a special financial aid guide. Hofstra's guide lists its major sources of aid. Its catalog describes in more detail Hofstra's privately funded scholarships.

What forms will I need to apply for financial aid? The most commonly used form is the Free Application for Federal Student Aid, also known as FAFSA. This form is used to help you apply for federal financial aid. In addition, the form also provides the information needed for many state and college aid programs.

FAFSA is a free form. You will not be charged any fee to file this form.

The form asks for detailed information about your own background, your assets (as well as your family's), and sources of income. Some of this information must be provided by your parents. The information is used to estimate your Expected Family Contribution (EFC). Colleges then use this figure to determine your financial aid package.

Many colleges have their own financial aid forms, which you must file in addition to the FAFSA. In most cases, the college's form should be filed at the same time as your application for admission.

While PROFILE is not a free form, you can apply for a fee waiver. Contact the College Board, the financial aid office, or your high school counselor.

Recently, a number of schools have been using (and sometimes requiring) PROFILE, a form for students applying for non-federal need-based aid. The form is handled by the College Scholarship Service. You must pay a fee when filing this form for each college that requires it.

You should hear about your financial aid package about the same time you hear whether you have been accepted. If receiving financial aid is necessary for you to be able to attend a college, do not feel compelled to commit to that college until you understand how much financial aid will be available. The package you receive will help you compare the real costs to you of different colleges.

Saving for College

Your parents may have already started saving for college. Get advice from them about opening up your own account for college, buying savings bonds, and keeping your savings in a safe place.

If you haven't already started saving for college, start now. The sooner you start, the more you will have available, and the more flexibility you will have in choosing where you go. Even if you do not go to college, your savings can help pay for vocational training, or any of a number of things— a car, a down payment on a house, or even the money you need to start your own business!

How can I save for college? Do you babysit? Do you have a paper route, mow lawns, shovel snow, or run errands for neighbors? All of these are fairly easy ways to earn money. When you're in high school, more opportunities may open up in fast-food and other restaurants, grocery stores, department stores, gas stations, and so forth.

Earning money from a job certainly helps pay for college. In addition, colleges will probably be interested in your work record as well as your reasons for working.

Decide in advance that you will put a certain portion of what you earn into a college fund. You may also want to put another portion into savings for other reasons. Saving money is a great habit to develop—it will serve you well your whole life!

What you earn from working is not your only source for savings. Anytime you receive money from relatives or friends for a birthday or holiday present, you should put aside as much as possible for savings.

While the first place to put any money you save may be a savings account, you should look into other places too. Savings bonds and certificates of deposit (CDs) may give you a higher interest. But keep saving your money. You will be amazed at how quickly your savings can grow!

WHERE THERE'S A WILL, THERE'S A WAY

We have looked at ways to find money and ways to save. You should also look at ways of lowering your costs of college.

Special guidebooks and other resources are available that rate colleges based on their value.

How can I lower my costs? Compare actual costs. Look at colleges that can help you achieve your goals. Compare their reputations. Lesser known colleges may help you achieve your goals for less money, without sacrificing quality.

When you make your final decision about where to attend, look at the real cost of your choices. Consider your financial aid package and hidden costs (e.g., travel). For example, College A may cost $8,000 a year, but you get no financial aid. College B may cost $12,000 a year, but you get $5,000 a year in grants. At first, College B seems more expensive than College A. But because of the package, College B is less expensive.

Transfer programs that ensure that students can move directly into their junior year at a four-year college are often referred to as 2+2 programs.

Engineering science students at Hudson Valley Community College in New York can transfer into their junior year at four-year colleges such as Clarkson University, Rensselaer, and Union College.

Don't forget transfer programs. Many students who attend two-year colleges go on to study at four-year colleges. Transfer programs can help students make the move to a four-year program without missing a beat. If you attend the two-year college and then transfer directly into your junior year at the four-year college, you can save a lot of money your first two years. Yet you still earn the same bachelor's degree as students who went only to the four-year college!

Be persistent. As the saying goes, where there is a will, there is a way. With enough hard work and determination, you will be able to afford to go to a college of your choice.

The Big Picture: Paying for College

College Name: _____

Personal Savings: $_____

Personal Investments: $_____

Earnings from Work: $_____

Contribution from Parents: $_____

Gifts from Family and Friends: $_____

Awards: $_____

Local Scholarships: $_____

Other Resources: $_____

YOUR TOTAL RESOURCES: $_____

TOTAL COLLEGE COSTS (from Chapter 10 chart): $_____

(subtract) YOUR TOTAL RESOURCES: — $_____

HOW MUCH YOU NEED: $_____

(minus) Grants and Scholarships: — $_____

AMOUNT STILL NEEDED (e.g., Loans): $_____

12 How Does College Begin?

College will be a new experience for you. Like many new experiences, this one will be exciting, and perhaps a bit scary. You might wonder how you will know what to do—what happens first?

Colleges have a lot of experience helping students through those first several weeks. In fact, many colleges help students prepare long before they actually arrive on campus. Once you do arrive, you will find lots of people to help guide you.

Remember, too, that you won't be alone. After all, many other first-time college students will be sharing the experience with you!

How Do I Get Started?

College begins in full swing once you're accepted and you've made your final decision about where to go. Now you can focus your attention on going to college rather than getting into college. And once the college knows you're coming, it focuses its attention on you and your fellow classmates!

You will probably start to get a lot of mail from the college. Carefully read the information that you receive. You probably should file this mail with other important information that you have from and about the college.

Even though you're now ready and anxious to go, you still have several steps to take before your first class. You need to sign up for orientation, make arrangements to get to the college, find your way around campus, choose and sign up for your classes, and buy your books and supplies.

When you make your plans for getting to college the first time, try to think ahead to the end of the college year as well as to any other trips you might be taking—for instance, holiday and vacation travel. You may be able to save quite a lot of money with some careful planning.

In addition, if you plan to live on campus or away from home, you also have some packing and moving ahead of you. You may need to arrange for housing and finding a roommate, whether you live on or off campus (see Chapter 13). If you are living away from home, you need to decide how you will move your belongings and how you will travel. And regardless of where you are living, you need to look into the various food plans that the college offers and choose one that makes the most sense for you.

These steps take time—more, in fact, than you probably realize. Whatever steps you take, always try to take them either on or ahead of time!

What is orientation? Most colleges offer at least one orientation program for incoming students. Orientation programs are designed to "orient" you to the college—they show you your way around campus. They help you understand what steps you need to get started and when to take them. They also explain campus rules and regulations and inform you about important campus services.

Some colleges have orientation programs for parents that answer their important questions.

Larger colleges usually have more than one orientation program. Some programs are specifically aimed at freshmen. Others may be designed for transfer students. In some cases, you can sign up for your classes during orientation. If you have a choice of dates for orientation, sign up as soon as possible and for the earliest possible date. You will then have a better chance at getting the date and, in turn, the classes you want.

Some orientation programs are very specific. For instance, early in your freshman year, you should take a tour of the library so that you will be sure you know your way around.

Colleges may have more than one kind of program. Some may have programs that focus on certain majors. Other programs may be geared for selected groups of students, such as international students or students with disabilities.

Several colleges have special programs for new students. For example, freshmen at Colby College in Maine can participate in a Colby Outdoor Orientation Trip (COOT) the week before regular orientation. Small groups of new students—led by upperclass students, faculty members, or staff—get a taste of Maine. Trips may include canoeing in the Belgrade Lakes, shooting the rapids on the Penobscot River, hiking Mt. Katahdin, and working as a volunteer in Portland. Students who participate in these programs make new friends who help make their first days easier.

If you will be commuting to campus, drive the route ahead of time. See how long you need to get to and from campus during the time of day that you expect to be making the trip.

Finding your way. You may have already toured the campus when you first applied to college. Still, take time to learn your way around. You might even take another tour. Get a copy of the campus map. (You may already have one from materials you received.) Find the location of the important places: your room (if you plan to live on campus), parking, classroom buildings, the student union, the bookstore, the library, and the dining hall. Also find where student services are located.

Once you know where classes will be held, make a trial run. Be sure you know how to get from one class to another and how much time you need. On some campuses, classroom buildings can be pretty far apart. Be sure you have time to get from one class to the next and know the fastest route!

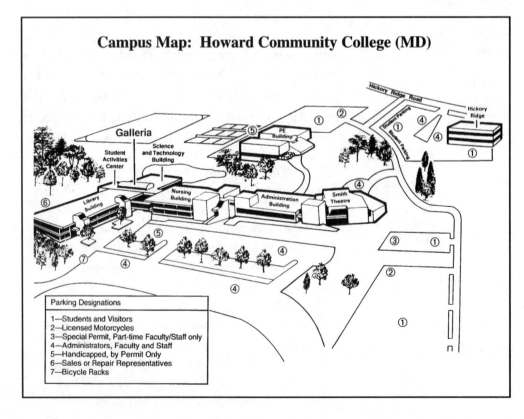

Campus Map: Howard Community College (MD)

Parking Designations

1—Students and Visitors
2—Licensed Motorcycles
3—Special Permit, Part-time Faculty/Staff only
4—Administrators, Faculty and Staff
5—Handicapped, by Permit Only
6—Sales or Repair Representatives
7—Bicycle Racks

WHAT IS PLACEMENT TESTING?

Many colleges test students to learn more about their skills. These placement tests, help colleges determine your level of skills. Colleges can then place you into classes that match your level. You do not pass or fail placement tests. You simply find out more about your current level.

The college may provide material that will help you prepare for placement tests.

Placement tests are most frequently given in math and English. However, colleges may test in other areas as well, especially foreign language and study skills. The tests are especially important in areas where the material you learn in one course is directly needed for the next course.

Open admissions colleges almost always give placement tests. These colleges do not restrict admission to the college. Therefore, they need a way of evaluating each student's skills. At most colleges (open, selective, and competitive), you may be excused from placement testing if your college entrance exam scores are high enough or if you have already taken certain high school or college classes.

Arrive on time for tests. Bring required materials, including a photo identification if needed. For math tests, find out what type of calculator you may use.

Many colleges give placement tests as part of their orientation program. Sometimes, you can walk right in to the placement office to take the test. Other times, you schedule your tests in advance.

In any case, take your placement tests as soon as you can. The sooner you learn the results, the more time you will have to determine how they affect the courses you select. In addition, many colleges will not let you sign up for courses until you have taken your placement tests.

REGISTERING FOR CLASSES

A lot of students do not really feel that they are college students until they have registered (signed up) for their first set of classes. While you have many decisions to make when you register, this period of time can be exciting—you're taking charge of your future!

You must register for classes before each term.

What is registration? In a nutshell, registration is the process of choosing the courses you would like to take, seeing that they all fit together into a good schedule, getting approval from the college to take those courses (and when you want), and then fine-tuning your schedule as needed. Placement tests help make sure you are taking courses at a level that is right for you. You should also have good information about whether courses you choose help you meet graduation requirements.

Once you have declared a major, usually in your sophomore year, you will be assigned an advisor who can help you until graduation. That advisor usually teaches in the program in which you are majoring.

Who can help me with registration? You may be assigned a freshman advisor to help you through your first registration. At many colleges, you will be assigned either a faculty member or someone from the advising or counseling center who will act as your advisor. Your advisor can help you select courses and build your schedule. Some colleges may assign you a student advisor as well, usually a junior or a senior who can help answer your questions about registration.

Advisors can help you choose the right courses in the right order so that you graduate on time. They can also help you prepare a planning form that you can use to keep track of the courses you have taken and those you still need to take in order to complete a major and to graduate.

Where do I learn about courses? The college catalog lists all the available courses, along with brief descriptions of each course. It tells you about general requirements that you must complete as well as specific requirements for your major.

The catalog is your contract with the college. The requirements listed *at the time you begin classes* will hold as long as you are a full-time student.

Sometimes, material taught in different sections is the same, especially in math classes. In other courses, content may be different. In freshman literature, for example, each section may focus on different readings.

The next handy tool is the schedule of classes. This schedule, which is revised each term, tells you when courses are offered and who teaches each course. In many cases, a course is offered at several different times. For example, precalculus may be offered at ten different times. Each of these classes is a section. The number of sections that are offered depends on the demand for the course. Professors may teach one or more sections.

You often see staff, instructor, TBD, *or* TBA *listed as the teacher. These mean the actual teacher was not known when the schedule was printed. TBD means "to be determined" and TBA means "to be announced."*

Class schedules list the name and number of each course (see next page). If the course has more than one section, each section is listed individually. The schedule lists the days and times each section is taught as well as its location—both the building and the room. The person teaching the course is listed whenever possible. Usually the schedule lists the number of credits or units you earn when you take the course.

Many classes are taught three times a week on Mondays, Wednesday, and Fridays for fifty minutes. These will be listed as MWF in a schedule. Classes that are taught twice a week, often for an hour and fifteen minutes, are usually held on Mondays and Wednesdays (MW) or Tuesdays and Thursdays (TTh).

If you took advanced high school courses or earned high scores on achievement and advanced placement tests, you may not have to take all of the general requirements courses.

How do I know which courses to take? You take some courses to meet general requirements. For example, most freshmen take composition or literature courses. The placement office can tell you which requirements you have met. It can also help you find the best level for certain subjects.

A prerequisite is a course that you are required (requisite) to take before (pre) taking another course.

The catalog tells you which courses are needed for different majors. It also tells you about course prerequisites. For example, you may need to take general psychology before taking developmental psychology. However, you may need to take both general psychology *and* statistics before you take an experimental psychology course.

Not all courses are offered every term. Some are offered once each year. Some are offered only every other year. Be aware of how often courses are offered when you make your selections.

The class schedule or catalog will have a guide to how courses are numbered.

Colleges have different ways of numbering courses. Courses below certain numbers may be remedial courses. Those with higher numbers may be restricted to juniors and seniors.

Course Numbering at Iowa State University

Course Numbers	Types of Courses
1-99	Courses have no credit toward degree
100-299	Mostly for freshmen and sophomores
300-499	Mostly for juniors and seniors
500-599	Mostly for graduate students, but qualified undergraduates can take the course
600-699	Only for graduate students

For example, Accounting 284 (Financial Accounting) is mostly for freshmen and sophomores and Accounting 316 (Business Law) is mostly for juniors and seniors.

How do I register for classes? Computers have made registration much easier. Before, almost everything was done by hand. The registrar (the person in charge of registration) and staff had lots of detail work now handled easily by computers.

Some colleges run registration on a first-come, first-serve basis. Other colleges decide the order. Usually seniors and juniors register first. Other students may be picked in alphabetical or some other order that is fair to all students over time. Colleges can usually accommodate students with special needs.

Try to register as soon as you can. Courses and sections fill up. You may get blocked from some courses because of space limitations. The earlier you register, the better your chances will be for getting the courses you want. You will also have more time to find other choices, if needed.

Most colleges have a time period when you can adjust your schedule. During this period you can add and drop courses. You may be able to switch sections as well, freeing up room for another class. Sometimes space opens up in a course that had been closed. If you are on a waiting list, you may be able to get into that class.

Ways to Register for Classes

Freshmen Orientation. Students register as part of orientation program.

Mail-In Registration. Students complete forms indicating courses and schedule they want; materials mailed to registrar and processed.

Computerized Registration. Students use computers linked to college's registration system; the Internet increases ability to register by computer; students get instant response about availability of classes.

Telephone Registration. Students either speak to college staff handling registration or use phone to link to college computer.

Walk-In or In-Person Registration. Students come directly to college to register; often used in last days before classes start.

How do I plan my schedule? When you first plan your schedule, you need to know what courses you want to take and when you want to take them. Sometimes certain sections or even entire courses are filled by students who register before you. You may not be able to get everything you want when you want it. Therefore you'll need back-up plans.

Many classes have required labs. Some classes and labs are scheduled together. In other cases, the two are independent of each other. Check which is the case for any labs you have.

When you plan your schedule, expect to be in class one hour for every credit you take. In addition, for every hour you are in class, you can expect to spend two to three hours studying and preparing homework. College students are usually considered to be full-time students if they take the equivalent of 12 or more credits per semester.

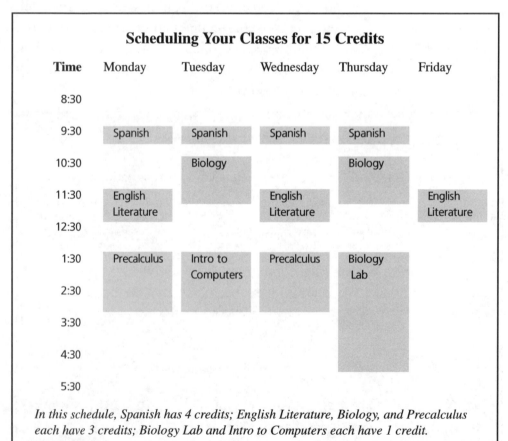

Scheduling Your Classes for 15 Credits

Time	Monday	Tuesday	Wednesday	Thursday	Friday
8:30					
9:30	Spanish	Spanish	Spanish	Spanish	
10:30		Biology		Biology	
11:30	English Literature		English Literature		English Literature
12:30					
1:30	Precalculus	Intro to Computers	Precalculus	Biology Lab	
2:30					
3:30					
4:30					
5:30					

In this schedule, Spanish has 4 credits; English Literature, Biology, and Precalculus each have 3 credits; Biology Lab and Intro to Computers each have 1 credit.

Nine Steps to Planning Your Schedule

1. **Gather Information.** Get your catalog and schedule of classes. Gather placement test scores and information from your advisor about how to register and which courses to take.

2. **Consider Your Needs and Preferences.** Would you prefer early or late classes? Be honest about your study skills and how they affect the number and kind of classes you take. Think about the time you need for work, commuting, or extracurricular activities.

3. **Balance Your Courses.** Think about the kind of homework the courses require (e.g., reading, writing, problem solving), your study strengths and weaknesses, and the difficulty of each course.

4. **Schedule Required Courses First.** Begin with courses that have the fewest sections. Do all you can to get into them. Schedule all other classes and activities around them. Next, schedule required courses that have many sections.

5. **Schedule Non-required Courses.** List these courses in order of preference. Go down the list until you find one that fits with your required courses and your preferred schedule.

6. **Prepare Required Information.** Write down information you need to register: course names and numbers, section numbers, and other related information.

7. **Be On Time.** Your planning is wasted if you do not register on time. If you stay ahead of schedule, you will get more classes you want and have time to solve problems that develop.

8. **Have a Back-up Plan.** Be ready with your next move if a course or a section is closed. Do not be shy about asking your advisor or others for help if you have trouble getting into a required class.

9. **Make a Final Schedule.** Once you have registered, create a final schedule that also includes your study time, work, meals, rest, and activities. Make extra copies for yourself.

Odds and Ends

Registering for classes is not the only step that you take before classes begin. Some other steps still remain.

Physicals, health forms, and insurance. You may need to get a physical examination before you begin college, especially if you plan to live on campus or are studying in certain fields. Colleges need to insure, for instance, that all students have been vaccinated for measles. You need to make sure you have proper health insurance, whether provided by you or by the college. If you have specific health concerns—for instance asthma or epilepsy—be sure that medical officials on campus are notified.

Your student ID can even save you money away from campus. For instance, you may get special rates when you travel if you can show a student ID.

IDs, permits, and forms. At some point early on, you will get a student identification (ID) card. You may need your ID to check out library materials, use the gym, and attend football games or other campus events. Your ID may even save you money with local shop owners.

Students who need parking permits should handle the paperwork before classes begin. Financial aid students have paperwork to complete each term. If you will be living in college housing, you have forms you should complete as soon as possible.

Get your books early! Once you know your schedule—and your sections—buy your books. Bookstores do not always have enough copies to go around. If you wait too long, the store may run out and have to reorder. Having your books early gives you a chance to get off to a strong start.

STARTING CLASSES

Little compares to the first day of classes! You already know this feeling: it combines excitement, nervousness, motivation, and a bit of uncertainty. But the day has arrived. You're ready to begin!

Double check the location of your classes. (Sometimes, classes are moved to different rooms or buildings.) In most cases, you can choose whatever seat you want. College classes usually do not have seating charts. Pick a seat close enough to the front of the room for you to hear clearly. You also want to be able to see anything the teacher writes on the chalkboard or shows on a screen (e.g., overhead transparencies, slides).

The syllabus often includes your teacher's office location, office hours, and phone number. It may also explain attendance and grading policies.

What is a syllabus? Most teachers hand out a course syllabus to students on the first day of class. The syllabus is an outline for the course. It often provides an idea of what will be taught each day of the class. It includes reading assignments and occasionally detailed homework assignments. The syllabus will also tell you when major projects such as papers are due and when you can expect to have major tests.

Students may check their own homework in math and go over especially difficult problems in class. The exercises may simply be given to help you practice— with solutions posted for you to check yourself. Chemistry and physics classes often work in the same way. Complete the work whether or not it is checked .

Is homework graded? It may or may not be. Homework in college is not quite the same as what you are used to now. Daily homework is often assigned to help you learn the lessons and prepare for each class. You usually do not have to turn in this kind of work, though teachers may check to see if you have completed it. However, larger assignments, including essays and research papers, may take several days or weeks to complete and may be an important part of your grade.

Your Studies Outside of Class

Exercises. More traditional homework involving solving problems or answering questions about reading material; questions often come from books; used often in math, statistics, accounting, chemistry, and physics.

Journals. Report you maintain on regular basis; may be creative writing, daily observations, or collection of data.

Papers. Brief exploration of certain topics; requires a certain amount of research, but usually from a limited number of sources; you may be asked to analyze a particular topic; can include informational writing, but can also include more creative writing and English compositions.

Problems. (See Exercises).

Research Papers. More formal and lengthier paper; usually requires you to use many sources of information; often involves formal use of footnotes, sources, and bibliography; usually very important to grade.

Discussion Groups. Extra session outside of regular class; smaller groups discuss topics related to class; may be run by professor or teaching assistant; all students expected to participate.

Lab Reports. While some labs are for practical experience, other labs require follow-up reports; these reports show that you are learning proper research methods and provide practice summarizing your findings.

Field Exercises and Labs. Required session outside of lecture class; provides students with chance to conduct experiments; used in natural sciences, computer science, some social sciences.

Staying on track. Keep up with your ongoing assignments. They are important on their own. They also help you prepare for tests and exams. Pay close attention to information about tests. Find out what kind of questions you can expect and how much they will count toward your grade.

Tests

Final. Important test given at the end of the term; test usually lasts two to three hours and may cover the entire course; grade often counts for one-third to one-half of grade for the course.

Hourly. Important test usually given once or twice during the term; test takes up entire class session; covers either the material from the start of term or material covered since the previous exam; grade may count for as much as one-third to one-half of grade for the course.

Midterm. Same as hourly, but offered halfway through the term; may count for up to one-half of grade for the course.

Pop Quiz. (See quiz). A brief test, usually not announced until the day it is given; used to check student progress with material, look for weak spots; also used to encourage students to keep up with daily work.

Quiz. A brief test; usually takes up less than half of the class; often focused on a specific amount of material; unlike pop quizzes, usually is announced in advance.

Refining your schedule. Once you have your class schedule and the syllabus for each course, you should refine your schedule. Create a big picture schedule for the term, accounting for not only your classes, but also tests, major assignments (e.g., research papers), and vacations.

Many people also use daily schedules. You can choose from different formats: formal daily or weekly planners, index cards, and a computerized calendar among them.

You should also create a weekly schedule with more detail. In the weekly schedule you can add in more information, for example, times that you meet with study groups, play sports, rehearse for a performance, or meet with a club. If you have any special events or meetings (for example, a guest lecture or a meeting with your advisor), you can add them as well to your weekly schedule.

Some colleges even offer credit/no credit courses. These are often experimental courses, some even taught by other students. No one is graded. You earn credits toward graduation, but not toward your major or general requirements.

Some professors require freshmen to meet with them at least once in their office. A professor's office hours are for you—for questions, advice, and simply getting to know your professor.

How will I be graded? For the most part, courses are graded the same way as in high school, though the grade may depend on fewer projects or tests. You often receive letter grades, but in some cases percentages are used.

Many colleges allow you to take some courses on a pass/fail basis. You don't receive a grade other than to show that you passed or failed the course. Most pass/fail courses do not count toward your major. They encourage students to take challenging courses outside their main area of study, but without the pressure of being graded.

Getting extra help. All sorts of resources are available to you. Many students find that studying with others helps. You may want to team up with other students early in the term to form a study group that meets regularly to go over class notes, homework, and reading assignments. Study group members can help each other with difficult portions of the course and help prepare for tests.

Most professors have office hours when you can see them about questions you have. You can look for learning labs run by departments or speak to your advisor about additional places to get help. In addition, colleges provide tutoring or other kinds of extra help. If you are unsure where to go, contact the Dean of Students office to be pointed in the right direction.

Enjoy the ride! All the new experiences that you will face, particularly in the first few weeks, can feel overwhelming at times. But they can also be fun—new learning opportunities, new people, new adventures. Seize them all!

13

WHAT HAPPENS AT COLLEGE?

Lots of activities and opportunities happen on a daily basis! Your studies, or course, are very important. But the many opportunities that take place outside your classes are also very important.

You'll meet new people; some will become lifelong friends. You'll also participate in many activities, some of them new to you. And you'll be challenged by others to expand your horizons.

In this chapter, we will look at student life—all that is available to do on campus when you are not in class. We will also look at what you can do to feel at home and take full advantage of college.

WHERE WILL YOU LIVE?

Some colleges require incoming freshmen to live on campus. Other colleges do not provide any housing—in this case, the decision is entirely yours. Still others give you a choice about where to live. Your decision is an important one.

Colleges often have drawings or lotteries to determine who gets to live in college housing or the order in which students pick their rooms.

In some cases, the college does not have enough housing for everyone. However, many students enjoy living off campus. Usually, the college sets aside enough space so that freshmen who want to live on campus can do so. Students who live off campus often rent apartments or rooms near the college. In addition, students attending a college near where they went to high school often live at home, at least during their freshman year.

Some larger rooms, called suites, have two or more small bedrooms and a larger shared living area.

What is a dormitory? Many college students live in college-run dormitories (often called dorms or residence halls). Dorms may provide housing for small groups or for hundreds of students. While some students (usually juniors or seniors) have their own room, most have roommates. Most rooms are doubles (two students), triples (three students), or quads (four students). Most dorm rooms provide you with a bed, a desk, a chair, a dresser, and a closet. You bring everything else!

Many dorm rooms now come with wiring to hook up your computer, also providing you with access to the Internet.

Some dorms have dining halls and study rooms in them. Most have lounges where students can spend free time just relaxing, watching television, playing games, or playing music. In most dorms, students share bathroom facilities with students from other rooms. Sometimes students on a floor have to share a telephone. In more and more cases, you can have your own phone in your room.

Living Arrangements in Dormitories

Male or Female. Students in the dorm are either all male or all female.

Coed by Floor. Both male and female students live in dorm; some floors are all male, some floors are all female.

Coed within Floor. Each floor has both male and female students.

Freshmen Only. Dorms focus on needs of new students.

International. Students in dorm are from countries all around the world, including Americans who would like this experience.

Honors. Dorm space is reserved for students in special honors programs; these dorms may have advantages (e.g., larger rooms, better location).

Alcohol-Free and Smoke-Free. Students sign pledge in which they agree to ban alcohol and cigarettes in dorm.

Colleges may also have area directors who oversee groups of dorms.

Deans of housing and directors of student life are responsible for making sure that campus housing is safe and comfortable. They and their staff oversee housing assignments, determining who lives where. They also assign roommates.

Who runs the dorms? The people who live in the dorms and are in charge of them are the dorm staff. Each dorm has a head resident who manages the dorm. Head residents are often seniors who have previously been members of the dorm staff. Head residents usually report to the dean of housing or the director of student life. They keep an eye out for the entire dorm and are informal counselors to students who live there.

Resident assistants or RAs live on each floor. They watch over all or part of a floor, depending on the size. They help students who are having problems, help settle disputes, and work to prevent problems. They also provide information, for example about fire drills, to students who live in the dorm. They usually report to the head resident.

Students may also have opportunities to live in fraternities, sororities, and other group housing, discussed later.

What other types of housing are available?

Many colleges have student apartments, both on and off campus. Unlike dorm rooms, apartments have their own bathrooms and kitchens. Some colleges maintain apartments to ensure a steady supply of student housing. College-run apartments usually go first to married students, graduate students, and upperclassmen.

Students can also find apartments and other homes on their own. In these situations, students make their own arrangements.

When you live off campus, you need to find your own roommate. Many colleges have student referral programs that help students find other students to be roommates. Many cities also have programs that help students find both off-campus housing and roommates.

How do I get a roommate? If you plan to live on campus, the college will send you special forms to complete. The forms include questions about your personal likes and dislikes and the kind of person with whom you might want to share a room. For example, the form might ask if you prefer to study with music playing or with no background noise. The college tries to match you with a roommate who has similar preferences.

The college usually takes responsibility for matching freshmen with their roommates. After that, you can continue with the same roommate, find one on your own, or have one chosen at random. As a freshman, you may be allowed to room with someone you already know. Other colleges want you to room with someone you do not know so that you will get to meet new people.

You have adjustments to make even if you live at home. Your relationship with your family changes. You also need to make sure you stay connected to the campus.

Many students must learn to make adjustments in getting along with their roommates. Learning to make these adjustments is an important part of the college experience. The dorm staff, advisors, and the dean of students are available to help you.

Of course, you can buy certain supplies after you arrive on campus.

What should I take with me to college? A lot of what you need depends on how far from home you will be going. If you are able to get home easily on weekends or even during the week, you can always pick up things that you forget. But if you are going to college far from home, you need to think through more carefully how you will pack.

Students often overlook the need to have good sound sleep. Pack a comfortable pillow or two—and a favorite blanket if you want.

For many students, going away to college is the first major time they have gone away from home. Items that you are used to having around—as simple as toothpaste and shampoo—now become your responsibility. Besides basics such as clothing, toiletries, and medicine, you will probably want to bring things that make you feel at home or which you can use for rest and recreation. These may include some favorite music, an inexpensive tape or CD player (and headphones!), favorite books, and athletic gear (e.g., a tennis racket or a baseball glove).

You may want to split the cost of certain items (e.g., a small refrigerator) with your roommate.

Your college may send a list of suggested supplies as well as optional items you can rent. Talk with your roommate to coordinate who will bring larger items such as a CD player or a rug.

Packing the Basics

College dictionary
Thesaurus
Computer and printer
  (or typewriter)
Calculator
Calendar
Daily planner
Good desk lamp
Supplies (pens, highlighters, etc.)

Alarm clock
Backpack or knapsack
Comfortable pillows and linens
Laundry bag or basket
Raincoat or poncho
Radio, tape or CD player
Address book
Postage stamps
Toiletries (shampoo, comb, etc.)

Together, fraternities and sororities are known as the Greek community or as the Greeks. The name of each organization consists of two or three letters of the Greek alphabet. For example, ZBT, or Zeta Beta Tau, is one of many fraternities. AKA, or Alpha Kappa Alpha, is one of many sororities.

What are fraternities and sororities? You may have a chance to join a fraternity or sorority. These are national membership organizations that offer opportunities for strong friendships, development of leadership skills, and participation in athletic, social, and community events. They set up chapters at various colleges. Fraternities are for males and sororities are for females. (A few individual chapters are coed.) Many colleges have both, though some do not permit them.

Many chapters operate houses on or near campus and provide housing for members who pay room charges. Each house may provide room for a few dozen members. Some chapters require their members to live in the house; others do not.

The process of recruiting new members is often called rushing.

Fraternities and sororities are not groups anyone can join. In most cases, you must be invited to become a brother (fraternity) or sister (sorority). You then go through many steps, during which time you are a pledge. The process of joining (called pledging) places significant demands on your time—all at a time when you are still trying to adjust to college life. Some colleges will not allow you to pledge until you have completed one or more terms.

An entire dorm may be set up as a cultural center. In addition, cultural centers may be located within dorms or be set up as independent locations on campus where students can gather.

What are cultural centers? Many colleges have centers where students can share their interest in particular cultures, whether or not they are from that cultural background. At the University of Massachusetts in Amherst, you will find several cultural centers, including the Martin Luther King Cultural Center, the Hispanic Cultural Center, the United Asia Cultural Center, and the Native American Cultural Center.

THE STUDENT UNION

While not all colleges have a separate student union, most have some sort of student center that serves the same purpose.

The student union is one of the first places you should find when you get to campus. The student union is an important place for students to gather.

Meals and books. Many students unions have places to eat, including regular dining halls and other places open late at night. The student union is also where you may find the campus bookstore. You can buy textbooks and other class materials at the bookstore. You can also find other books and magazines, college clothing (jerseys, sweatshirts, and other items with the college name and logo on them), and many other items.

Getting mail. As a student, you may have your own mailing address at the college. The mail is sent to a central location, often the student union, where you have a mailbox and key. Larger colleges may have several locations where mail is received and sent out.

The student union sometimes houses the campus infirmary and other health services.

Services. The student union may also be the place where most student services are located. You might find counseling, advising, placement, and employment offices there. The members of the administration who coordinate student activities (concerts, clubs, intramural sports) may have their offices in the union. You will also find meeting rooms, lounges, and even small performance sites for plays and concerts.

Larger student unions may have even more: hair stylists, travel agencies, banking services, shops, game rooms and bowling alleys, and even movie auditoriums and hotel rooms.

CLUBS AND ORGANIZATIONS

When you go to college, you will be able to choose from dozens of different clubs and organizations. In fact, at some colleges, you will be able to choose from hundreds of groups.

You may decide to play a sport, either with an official team or an intramural team. You may want to get active with a college publication such as the campus newspaper or literary magazine. You may also be interested in student government.

Academic organizations. Many groups are made up of students who share an academic interest. For example, a biology club might bring leading biologists to campus for guest lectures or plan a field trip to study plant life in a nearby forest. In addition, academic organizations often help their members find jobs.

Religious organizations. You'll find many groups of students who share a common faith. These groups often organize special worship services, discussion groups, and other religious and social events. For example, the Newman Club serves the needs of Roman Catholic students while Hillel serves the needs of Jewish students. Campus groups often have ties to the local community.

 **Performance organizations.** Most colleges have a campus-wide choir, often called a glee club. You may also be able to play with a marching band, an orchestra, or a small chamber group. Colleges also have theater groups, smaller singing groups, dance companies, and bands. Some are ongoing while others come together on short notice.

Service organizations. Many organizations are formed to serve the campus or the surrounding community. For example, Big Brother and Big Sister programs match college students with kids from the community. College students often help build homes in the community or volunteer at nearby shelters. They also hold lots of special events, such as dance-a-thons to raise money for groups like the Muscular Dystrophy Association. Service groups also run programs on campus. For instance, some groups provide an escort service so that students do not have to walk alone across campus at night.

Social organizations. Many groups provide ways for students with similar interests or backgrounds to get together for fun. Some might be based on students' hometowns. For example, Grambling State University in Louisiana has a group for students from Michigan. Other groups center around activities, for example, a chess club, a debate club, a line dancing club, and a rock climbing club.

Political organizations. Students who share the same views on politics and issues often have their own organizations. For example, you might find clubs for both Young Republicans and Young Democrats at many colleges.

Support organizations. Some groups help students share problems or concerns that they have. These groups can provide opportunities to voice their views, and help students find and give both comfort and advice. For example, you may find groups that provide support for students with HIV and AIDS, or for students with other physical or personal challenges.

Some of the Student Organizations at Auburn University

Choral Groups

Concert Choir
Gospel Choir
University Singers
Men's Chorus
Women's Chorus

Bands

Marching Band
Symphonic Band
Concert Band
Basketball Pep Band
Music Ensembles
Jazz Ensembles
Majorettes and Flags

Theatrical Groups

The Telfair Peet Theatre
AU Summerstage
Theatre Upstairs

Military Organizations

Angel Flight
Arnold Air Society
Blue and Gold Society
Kadettes
Mariners
Semper Fidelis Society
Steerage

Many Departmental Clubs
Many Professional Clubs
Many Honor Societies

Service Organizations

Alpha Phi Omega
Campus Civitan Club
Circle K
Project Uplift

Religious Organizations

AU B'nai B'rith Hillel
Auburn Christian Fellowship
Baptist Campus Ministry
Campus Crusade for Christ
Catholic Student Organization
Eastern Orthodox Christian
    Association
Muslim Association
St. Dunstan's Chapel

Special Interest

Amnesty International
Amateur Radio Club
Auburn College Republications
Auburn Planesmen R/C Club
AU Libertarians
Best Buddies
Black Student Union
Chinese Student Association
Environmental Awareness Org.
Habitat for Humanity
International Students Org.
Korean Student Association
Rugger Huggers
Tigerettes/Tiger Hosts

Many Sports Clubs

Extra! Learn All About it!!

College newspapers need reporters, editors, columnists, photographers, advertising coordinators, and publishers. At many colleges, some students can get paid for their work.

Another way you can get active at college is to work on a student publication. Most colleges have at least one campus newspaper. The paper comes out once a week on some campuses. And at larger colleges, the paper is often published daily.

Campus newspapers provide information about important issues on campus; a summary of the news both on and off campus; reviews of films, concerts, and plays; sports results; and calendars of upcoming events. They also have editorial pages that print the ideas and opinions of both the newspaper staff and the college community.

Many colleges have literary magazines that give students a chance to publish stories, essays, drawings, poems, and photographs. Colleges also have student yearbooks. Other publications may be available depending on student interest.

WNUR-FM is the student-run radio station at Northwestern University in Illinois. On the air 24 hours a day, it is the largest student-run station in the country. Mt. Hood Community College broadcasts KMHD—Portland, Oregon's all-jazz radio station.

In addition to publications, many colleges have student-run radio stations. These stations may combine music with news, issue-oriented shows, and call-in talk shows. Faculty, staff, and members of the community often get involved as well, frequently hosting their own shows.

Students have lots of other ways to communicate with each other. Some colleges run public-access television programs, providing students with both on-air time and behind-the-scenes experience. Computers provide an increasingly important way to communicate. Many colleges even provide students with the ability to set up their own home pages within the college or on the Internet.

Sports at College

Sports are an important part of campus life. Most colleges have college-run teams in a variety of sports; these teams play teams from other colleges. Most colleges are organized into groups called conferences. Teams within the conference play each other often and develop long-term rivalries.

Official teams with the top players are often called varsity teams. Many colleges have junior varsity teams as well. These often feature athletes who are freshmen or sophomores or students who are waiting for openings on the varsity teams. Teams play according to rules established by groups that set policies for college participation in sports.

The NCAA has strict rules about how athletes are recruited, the financial aid they can receive, their academic performance, and their conduct on and off the field. See your counselor or advisor for more information.

The National Collegiate Athletic Association (NCAA) is the most prominent group overseeing college participation. The NCAA divides colleges and conferences into several different divisions. Colleges that have the largest or highest quality teams usually play in Division I. Colleges may be in different divisions for different sports. For example, a college might play football in either Division I-AA or II but basketball in Division I.

The West Coast Conference is an NCAA conference made up of eight colleges that play each other in basketball and other sports. Six members of the conference are in California (Loyola Marymount University, Pepperdine University, Saint Mary's College, Santa Clara University, University of San Diego, and University of San Francisco). The other two members are the University of Portland (OR) and Gonzaga University (WA).

What academic requirements do athletes have?
In recent years, the standards for playing college sports have become more and more strict. In short, athletes are expected to maintain certain grade point averages in order to play for a team. In many cases they must also have a certain score on college entrance examinations. Organizations like the NCAA establish these guidelines and review them regularly. In addition, individual conferences or colleges may set even higher standards.

What opportunities are available for women?
Over the past twenty years, opportunities for women to play varsity sports have skyrocketed. More and more women are also finding jobs as sports writers, broadcasters, and commentators. Sports like swimming, diving, tennis, and track and field have provided opportunities for many years. More recently, basketball and soccer have started to catch up. Opportunities will continue to grow, especially as more scholarships become available to top female athletes.

Time commitment. In order to play on a varsity team, you must make a huge time commitment, even to keep in shape during the off-season. You must be very self-disciplined and organized to play a varsity sport while maintaining your grades. Play on the team if you have the desire, the ability, and the time. Do not be pressured by others and do not sacrifice your academic performance.

College athletics are also important at two-year colleges, which offer most of the same sports as the four-year colleges. Among the major groups overseeing athletics is the Junior College Athletic Association (JUCO).

You can also be involved with college athletics without having to play for a team. You may have the chance to be an assistant trainer or a student manager.

Can I play on other types of teams? At most colleges, anyone can join an intramural team for fun. Intramural teams are made up of groups of students within the college, often organized into leagues. They play most games against each other. For example, different fraternities and sororities may have their own intramural teams. A team may also be made up of students from a specific dorm, a specific club, or any other group of students who want to play together. Colleges have their own rules about how intramural sports are organized.

In some cases, students who have an interest in a particular sport form a club. They may play clubs from other colleges or clubs from the community. Sports clubs are often formed for sports that are not covered by college-run varsity teams and that do not have enough interest on campus to set up a league of intramural teams.

Sports at Temple University (PA)

Varsity Sports. Includes baseball (M), basketball (M/F), crew (M/F), fencing (F), field hockey (F), football (M), golf (M), gymnastics (M/F), lacrosse (F), soccer (M/F), softball (F), tennis (M/F), track and field (M/F), volleyball (F).

Intramural Sports and Events. Aerobics (Hi, Low, Step), basketball, 3-3 basketball, flag football, floor hockey, foul shooting, golf tournament, indoor and outdoor soccer, softball, volleyball, outdoor volleyball, 5-mile run, net night.

Sports Clubs. Aerobic development, bowling, disabled sports, karate, lacrosse (M), rugby, swimming, Tae Kwon Do, volleyball (M), wheelchair basketball.

M—male, F—female, M/F—male and female

School spirit. Sports have a way of bringing people together at many colleges. In one sense, they physically bring people together—athletes, cheerleaders, the band, and spectators made up of students, faculty, staff, alumni, parents, and members of the community all gather in the same place to support the team and the college.

They also bring people together emotionally. The school spirit that is generated by sports is very important to a lot of colleges. Of course, sports are not the only source of school spirit. All of the other activities and organizations are also very important to how the people at a college feel about themselves and their college community.

As at high schools, most colleges also have school colors (usually two) that are used in uniforms for athletes, cheerleaders and others. Most mascots display these colors.

Mascots and nicknames. Most colleges have figures, or mascots, that symbolize the college. The name of the mascot often becomes the nickname of the college and its sports teams. One of the best known mascots is the Nittany Lion of Penn State University.

Certain mascots and nicknames are popular for teams because they represent strength or bravery. Many colleges pick mascots and nicknames that have special meaning based on the college's name (the Bonnies of St. Bonaventure University in New York), history (the Minutemen of the University of Massachusetts), or area of emphasis (the Miners of New Mexico Institute of Technology).

The mascots appear in all sorts of places—mugs, bumper stickers, sweatshirts and other clothing, notebooks, and so forth. They may also appear live at sporting events and other campus activities, sometimes played by students in costume.

It's All in the Name!

State	College or University	Nickname/Mascot
Alabama	University of Alabama	Crimson Tide
Alaska	Univ. of Alaska—SE	Humpback Whales
Arizona	Arizona State University	Sun Devils
Akansas	Southern Arkansas Univ.	Mule Riders
California	California State Univ.—Monterey Bay	Sea Otters
Colorado	Colorado School of Mines	Orediggers
Connecticut	Connecticut College	Camels
Delaware	University of Delaware	Blue Hens
Florida	Stetson University	Hatters
Georgia	Oglethorpe University	Stormy Petrels
Hawaii	University of Hawaii	Rainbow Warriors
Idaho	University of Idaho	Vandals
Illinois	Knox College	Prairie Fire
Indiana	Purdue University	Boilermakers
Iowa	St. Ambrose University	Bees
Kansas	Wichita State University	Shockers
Kentucky	Centre College	Praying Colonels
Louisiana	Univ. of SW Louisiana	Ragin' Cajuns
Maine	University of Maine	Black Bears
Maryland	University of Maryland	Terrapins
Massachusetts	Brandeis University	Judges
Michigan	University of Michigan	Wolverines
Minnesota	Concordia College	Cobbers
Mississippi	Mississippi Valley State U.	Delta Devils
Missouri	Univ. of MO—St. Louis	Rivermen
Montana	MT St. Univ.—Northern	Northern Lights

The University of California at Santa Cruz has an unusual mascot—the banana slug! Student demand and a strong publicity campaign led to the previous mascot, the sea lion, being replaced in 1986 by the banana slug.

It's All in the Name!

State	College or University	Nickname/Mascot
Nebraska	Nebraska Wesleyan Univ.	Plainsmen
Nevada	U. of Nevada—Las Vegas	Runnin' Rebels
New Hampshire	New England College	Pilgrims
New Jersey	Jersey City State College	Gothic Knights
New Mexico	University of New Mexico	Lobos
New York	Yeshiva University	Maccabees
North Carolina	Univ. of North Carolina	Tar Heels
North Dakota	Jamestown College	Jimmies
Ohio	University of Toledo	Mud Hens
Oklahoma	University of Oklahoma	Sooners
Oregon	University of Oregon	Ducks
Pennsylvania	University of Pennsylvania	Quakers
Rhode Island	Providence College	Friars
South Carolina	Univ. of South Carolina—Coastal Carolina	Chanticleers
South Dakota	SD School of Mines	Hardrockers
Tennessee	Vanderbilt University	Commodores
Texas	Texas Christian University	Horned Frogs
Utah	Westminister College	Parsons
Vermont	University of Vermont	Catamounts
Virginia	University of Richmond	Spiders
Washington	Evergreen State College	Geoducks
West Virginia	Marshall University	Thundering Herd
Wisconsin	St. Norbert College	Green Knights
Wyoming	University of Wyoming	Cowboys
District of Columbia	Georgetown University	Hoyas

Among the most popular college nicknames are the Tigers, the Bulldogs, the Pioneers, the Crusaders, the Wildcats, the Panthers, and the Lions. But easily the most popular nickname of all is the Eagles, used by over 50 colleges!

STUDENT GOVERNMENT

One of the most important student organizations at any college is the student government. Student governments have officers and people in charge of important committees. Some have a senate or an assembly as well.

Each class (freshman, sophomore, etc.) may have its own officers and committees. The senior class officers play an important role in planning any special events that will be held during graduation week.

At most colleges, all of the students vote for the president, vice president, and treasurer. They may also vote for other officers and committee heads. In some cases, students elect representatives from different student groups: dormitories, fraternities, sororities, commuters, and other groups. In these cases, the students within each group vote for their representative.

What Does Student Government Do?

Distributes Money to Student Organizations. The student government budget comes from student activity fees and fundraising events. Student government decides how money will be spent, including how much goes to different clubs and organizations.

Sponsors Special Events. Student government plays an important role in a college's social and cultural life. It sponsors concerts, guest speakers, dances, festivals, barbeques, debates, and other events.

Works with Faculty and Administration. The student government can influence areas of the college such as academic or student policies, new programs and services, and changes to existing services. Students often serve on important college committees.

Oversees Certain Parts of the Student Code of Conduct. Disputes between students are often heard by student judiciary boards. These boards may deal with other violations, including honor code violations. (Many honor codes deal with honesty, cheating, and other student behavior.)

SPECIAL EVENTS

Many colleges hold a Homecoming weekend in the fall. Alumni are invited back to share in special events. The weekend often includes an important football game, a big dance, dinners, and, in many cases, a parade.

In addition to your ongoing activities, you can participate in special events on a regular basis. Each week brings lectures, seminars, concerts, and other events. Some are sponsored directly by the college. Many others are sponsored by student clubs and academic departments.

For example, during a typical week, you may be able to attend lectures by a politician discussing foreign aid and a biologist explaining changes in our national parks. You may attend a debate on gun control or a symposium in which experts from many different fields discuss the media's role in covering trials.

During the same week, a rock band may play a concert on campus, an English professor may read a collection of newly written poems, and the art gallery on campus may open a special exhibit of paintings and sculptures created by students.

Meanwhile, the Business Club may have the head of a software company meet with its members to discuss marketing products on the Internet. Three of the religious organizations on campus may sponsor an interfaith dinner. The Outing Club may sponsor a Woodsman's Tournament with teams from around the state. And one of the service clubs may hold a dance marathon to raise money for a homeless shelter.

Colleges publish weekly and daily calendars of all these events. Be sure to be on the lookout for information about these events. Try to fit some of them into your regular schedule.

Feeling Like You Belong

At some point, you might find yourself feeling somewhat lost or lonely. You may feel overwhelmed by the amount of work, the difficulty of the work, or all the choices you have. These reactions can make you feel like you chose the wrong college or don't belong in college at all.

Try to relax and take positive steps! You wouldn't be the first student to feel that way—nor will you be the last. So, remember, you're not alone.

Are you taking care of yourself? Going to class all day, studying all night, and fitting in activities and special events—not to mention taking time to make new friends or to handle a job or other responsibilities—may make you feel like you are burning the candle at both ends. Be sure you get enough sleep. Being rested will help you make more efficient use of your time. You will also lower your chances of getting sick.

Be sure to eat properly and get exercise. The healthier you are, the more easily you will be able to handle your commitments.

You are better off asking for help early and then finding you don't need it than waiting until your problems get worse. Don't be shy! Colleges offer many services because lots of students need them—not just you!

Are you having trouble with your classes? Don't waste a moment. Get some help. You have all sorts of choices open to you. They include getting a tutor, working with a study group, going to a learning lab, and improving your study skills. You can talk to your advisor, the counseling office, your professors, members of the dorm staff, or even other students. Don't delay, however. If you tackle your obstacles the moment you encounter them, then you can take full control of them quickly.

Are you spread too thin? One problem a lot of students face is taking on too many commitments. The extra activities and special events make your college experience more complete. Remember, however, that your commitment to your studies must take first priority.

But don't go in the other direction either. Your classes will (and should) take up much of your time. But with careful planning and self-discipline, you should be able to enjoy college activities and special events as well.

Many colleges offer classes that help you learn to manage your time. Check with the counseling, advising, or entry services office.

Manage your time by developing weekly and daily schedules that work for you. Schedule time for your studies and your job, if you have one. Also schedule time for friends and recreation. Make necessary adjustments, but stick to your overall schedule. The same people who can help you with your classes can help you learn to manage time.

Are you feeling lonely or homesick? A lot of freshmen and even sophomores have to adjust to being away from home and starting in a new place where they don't know anyone. Sometimes you are simply caught offguard. You have been so excited about starting college that it never occurred to you that you could miss home and old friends. You may be worried about what others will think and try to hide how you're feeling.

Going to college can be like going to summer camp for the first time. A lot of people feel lonely, but only until they get the hang of it!

Being lonely or homesick is natural. But if it gets to you in a way that interferes with your studies or your enjoyment of college, then talk to someone. Speak to a counselor, a favorite professor, your advisor, or minister. They can provide you with lots of tips for feeling more at home.

What can I do to fit in? Remember why you picked your college in the first place. Focus on the positive. Find things that make you glad you're there—a favorite class, a place on campus where you like to spend time, an activity you enjoy.

Suppose you don't get the part you want in a play. Find other ways to be involved— building sets, helping with publicity, etc.

Become active. Do not be discouraged if your first choices are not available. The more you participate, the more likely you are to make new friends and feel like you are fitting in.

Look for events that bring the college together. Football and soccer games provide opportunities early on in the year. Try to hook into school spirit. Colleges have events like winter carnivals and spring festivals that involve the entire campus and will give you a sense of belonging.

And, as we've noted before, remember that you can change your mind. If you have addressed the issues discussed here and still do not feel like you belong, you can always consider opportunities at other colleges. What is important, as always, is that you recognize college as an opportunity. You are in charge of making it the best you can. If you take charge, your college experience—wherever you go—will be a rewarding one that will shape your dreams and plans for the rest of your life!

Each winter brings the Big Red Freakout to Rensselaer Polytechnic Institute in New York. The Freakout is more than a hockey game in February. Thousands dress in red or red and white paint, and bring the loudest noisemakers they can find to the game. Through television, this event is shared nationwide with alumni and fans.

14

WHAT SHOULD I DO NOW?

You should plan for your future! Whatever age you are and whatever your grade is in school, now is a great time to start looking ahead.

Everything we have discussed in this book up to now boils down to a few basic points: know who you are, develop your skills, make your decisions with care, and follow your heart.

College may or may not be the best path for you. But you can always improve your skills. And you have the opportunity to learn who you are and to make decisions about your future—decisions that will help you achieve your goals!

TAKE A PICTURE OF YOURSELF

In Chapter 8, we looked at steps you can take to know yourself better when you're ready to apply to college. You take these steps when you are trying to find the best fit between you and different colleges.

By the time you are a junior or senior in high school, you have created much of the record that affects where you will be accepted. But in the school years before, you have time to make changes. You need good information—and you begin by getting to know yourself better. The steps you take to get a picture of yourself are a little different than before.

One of the most important things you can do is become aware of what interests you. You don't need to set long-term goals yet, but you can start exploring them.

If there are subjects that come naturally to you and that you like, challenge yourself to go further with them. If other subjects are harder, try to learn why you are having trouble with them. Talk to your parents, teachers and guidance counselors.

Look at your abilities now. Ask where they should be if you are going to accomplish your goals. For example, if you want to be a journalist, you need strong writing skills. If you don't have them now, you will need to work to improve them.

You have the time *now* to make these changes. And because you have that time, more doors of opportunity are still open to you!

Finding a role model. Some people cannot even imagine going to college. Perhaps no one in your family has gone or you feel that you are not strong enough as a student to go to college. Concerns about money might stop you from even thinking about going to college.

Mentors are like role models. A role model may be someone you know or someone you admire from far away. A mentor is someone who works side-by-side with you.

Finding a role model is a great way for you to overcome these concerns. Even if you know that you are headed to college, a role model can help you. A role model is someone whom you admire and who has been successful in ways that you too would like to be successful.

We often pick athletes or celebrities as role models. But the best role models are often relatives, teachers, coaches, clergy, and others close to our daily lives.

The best role models are people with backgrounds similar to yours who can inspire you to go after your dreams. They can share with you what they did to achieve their goals and to overcome any obstacles in their way. They can give you ideas about steps that you should now be taking.

The Chamber of Commerce is made up of local businesses and professionals who care about their community. Similar groups include the Jay-Cees, the Rotary Club, and the Kiwanis.

Your school and a nearby college may have set up a program that can put you in touch with a college student or alumnus. See your guidance counselor. The local Chamber of Commerce or other business groups in town may have mentoring programs. These programs give you a chance to work alongside someone in a career area that may be of interest to you.

The University of New Mexico publishes the UNM Minority Resource Guide, which includes programs aimed at students from local school districts. For example, the Mentorship Program teams up African-American college students with African-American elementary school students.

EXPLORING YOUR OPTIONS

In Chapter 2, we discussed colleges and career opportunities. We looked at ways you can explore specific careers. And you can take many of these steps at any time, beginning today!

Learning about careers can help you in several ways. You can make choices that will improve your opportunities later. For example, if you are interested in being a veterinarian, you can choose courses in high school that will help you get into colleges with good veterinary programs. To improve your chances even more, you can take on related projects and work. For instance, you could get jobs in a veterinarian's office, on a farm, or even at a kennel—something that will have you working with animals.

Another advantage of exploring careers early is that you may be able to rule things out. In this same example, you might discover through the courses that you take or jobs you have, that you really are not interested in being a veterinarian. You are better off finding this out early rather than when you have already started at college.

When Gina Dounelis was a ballet student in middle school, she developed an interest in becoming a physical therapist. Over the last few years, she has learned more about the field and about which colleges offer programs in physical therapy. She is now taking the high school courses that she needs to get into these programs. Meanwhile, she works with her high school's athletic trainer as an assistant trainer for her school's football team.

CHECKING YOUR STUDY HABITS AND SKILLS

Now is the time to take a close look at your study habits and skills. Evaluate what you do well and where an improvement could make a difference.

Study habits. Start with your study habits, thinking: When? How? What? Where?

Believe it or not, sometimes you can study too hard. If you study long hours, be sure you take study breaks. Get up, stretch, walk around, take a few moments regularly to refresh yourself.

When do you study? Do you study when you first come home from school, late at night, early in the morning, on weekends? When do you complete your homework: when it is first assigned or at the last minute? When do you work on big projects?

How do you organize yourself? How do you keep track of homework assignments? Do you write them down in an easy-to-find place? How do you organize school papers and class notes? Are the subjects all jumbled together or is each organized?

What do you need to study? Do you have the books, supplies, and equipment you need? Do you play music or the television, or tune out all noise?

Where do you study? Do you study at a desk in your room, lying down on your bed or the floor, or somewhere else? Have you ever experimented with different surroundings?

No single study method works best for everyone. If you know your habits, then you can figure out what works best for you and what doesn't work at all. You can experiment with different ways of studying. What works for others may not work for you. And what works for you in some subjects may not work for you in other subjects.

Study skills. Your study skills are not quite the same as your habits. For example, you might be in the habit of taking notes during class. But your notetaking skill may need work. Your notes may be unclear and hard to follow. They might be so sketchy that they don't help you when you review for a test. Or they might be so detailed that you use lots of time that could be spent elsewhere. Then when you review for a test you need to wade through everything rather than just key points.

Perhaps you have excellent study habits, but weak study skills. For a while, your habits may have helped you to good results in school. But as your subjects get more difficult, you need to strengthen your skills. Even if you already have good skills, you should always look for ways to improve them.

You may do well on essay tests and short-answer tests, but struggle with multiple-choice tests. In this case, you would want special help that focuses on multiple-choice tests.

Your school counselor and teachers can help you figure out which areas need the most work. If you look at yourself honestly, you too will be able to figure out the skills that need your attention. For example, you might do well remembering what your teachers have said in class, but struggle to remember anything you read in a textbook. In this case, you might need help learning how to get the information you need out of a book.

Many community and church groups provide tutoring services for students who might not otherwise have access to such help.

In addition to getting help from people at your school, you may want to take special courses that focus on study skills. Tutors can often give you one-on-one attention that is very helpful.

You may find companies that specialize in study skills. Videos and television, software programs, and all sorts of guides and books can also help you build your study and test-taking skills.

Important Study Skills

Listening. How closely do you pay attention when your teacher or class-mates are speaking? Do you jump to conclusions before they are done? How well do you remember what was said?

Vocabulary. Do you understand most of the words you read? Do you keep a dictionary nearby? (How often do you use it?!) Do you try to figure out what words mean before looking up their definition? How often do you practice using new words?

Reading Speed and Comprehension. How long do you need to read your assignments? Do you need the same amount of time for fiction and text? Do you understand most of what you read? When you read a text-book, how often do you skim the material first, then go back and read it more closely? Do you answer sample problems and review questions?

Memory. How well do you remember what you have heard or read? How long are you able to remember material? When you study for a test, do you feel like you are starting from the beginning?

Writing. Does writing come easily to you? Are there types of writing that you prefer (essays, stories, poems, reports, and so forth)? Are you organized when you work on a report? Do you know how to outline a report? Are you able to summarize your thoughts clearly?

Note Taking. Do you take very detailed notes? Do you have a way of highlighting important information? Do you copy over your notes? How often do you review them? Are they helpful when you study for a test?

Test Taking. Do certain types of tests (essay, short answer, matching, and so forth) come more easily to you than other types? Do you wait until the last minute to start studying for tests? Do you run out of time when you take tests? How do you prepare for tests?

Using Study Tools. How well do you know how to use the library? How comfortable are you with a dictionary, thesaurus, or other reference books? How are your skills with calculators, computers, and CD-ROM?

Read, read, read! Make reading a lifelong habit. Read to relax, read to learn, read to have fun. Try to read as much as possible between now and the time you go to college. Even if you are a senior who has already been accepted to college, you should continue to read as much as you can.

Be an active reader, not a passive one. Read to build your vocabulary. Read to learn information. Read to understand new ideas and complicated theories. Being a good reader is like being a good athlete or a good musician. All take practice and then more practice.

What if reading is hard? If you have a reading problem, deal with it right away! Maybe you missed out on certain skills when you were younger and have simply fallen behind. Or you may have a learning disorder, like dyslexia, which may be overcome with special training. Don't be shy or embarrassed. You are not alone. Speak to your parents, teacher, or counselor. Get the support you need. You'll be amazed at how quickly you can tackle most problems. Once you do, the world opens up in ways you cannot imagine!

Your teacher or counselor can add more recent books to this list. Also, the admissions office or English departments at colleges of interest to you may be able to provide other ideas. For many authors on this list, you can substitute other works they wrote.

Schools and colleges often put together reading lists suggesting books that students should read by the time they get to college. Most books on these lists are classics—they've stood the test of time. The books listed on the next pages are ones that appear frequently on suggested reading lists.

Most of the books listed here are fiction. You will probably want to add more poetry and drama to it, as well as philosophy, history, biography, and other nonfiction.

Read, Read, Read . . .

Author	Title
James Agee	A Death in the Family
Maya Angelou	I Know Why the Caged Bird Sings
Jean Anouilh	Becket
Jane Austen	Pride and Prejudice
Ray Bradbury	The Martian Chronicles
Charlotte Brontë	Jane Eyre
Emily Brontë	Wuthering Heights
Pearl Buck	The Good Earth
Thomas Bulfinch	The Age of Fables
John Bunyan	Pilgrim's Progress
Albert Camus	The Stranger
Lewis Carroll	Alice's Adventures in Wonderland
Willa Cather	My Antonia
Geoffrey Chaucer	The Canterbury Tales
Joseph Conrad	Lord Jim
James Fenimore Cooper	The Last of the Mohicans
Stephen Crane	The Red Badge of Courage
Daniel Defoe	Robinson Crusoe
Charles Dickens	A Tale of Two Cities
	David Copperfield
Fyodor Dostoyevsky	The Brothers Karamazov
Sir Arthur Conan Doyle	The Hound of the Baskervilles
Alexandre Dumas	The Count of Monte Cristo
Daphne DuMaurier	Rebecca
George Eliot	Silas Marner
	Middlemarch
Ralph Ellison	Invisible Man
Euripides	Medea
William Faulkner	As I Lay Dying

Read, Read, Read . . .

Author	Title
Henry Fielding	Tom Jones
F. Scott Fitzgerald	The Great Gatsby
Gustave Flaubert	Madame Bovary
Benjamin Franklin	The Autobiography of Benjamin Franklin
Hamlin Garland	Main-Travelled Roads
William Golding	Lord of the Flies
Alex Haley	Roots
Edith Hamilton	Mythology
Thomas Hardy	The Mayor of Casterbridge
Bret Harte	"The Luck of Roaring Camp"
Nathaniel Hawthorne	The Scarlet Letter
Ernest Hemingway	The Sun Also Rises
	The Old Man and the Sea
John Hersey	Hiroshima
Thor Heyerdahl	Kon-Tiki
Homer	The Iliad
	The Odyssey
Victor Hugo	Les Misérables
Aldous Huxley	Brave New World
Henrik Ibsen	A Doll's House
Washington Irving	The Sketch Book
Ken Kesey	One Flew Over the Cuckoo's Nest
Rudyard Kipling	Kim
Harper Lee	To Kill a Mockingbird
Sinclair Lewis	Babbitt
Jack London	The Call of the Wild
Bernard Malamud	The Natural
Herman Melville	Moby-Dick

Read, Read, Read . . .

Author	Title
Arthur Miller	The Crucible
Frank Norris	McTeague
John O'Hara	Appointment in Samarra
Eugene O'Neill	Long Day's Journey into Night
George Orwell	Animal Farm
Edgar Allan Poe	Tales ("Cask of Amontillado")
Erich Maria Remarque	All Quiet on the Western Front
J. D. Salinger	The Catcher in the Rye
Sir Walter Scott	Ivanhoe
William Shakespeare	Macbeth
	A Midsummer Night's Dream
George Bernard Shaw	Pygmalion
Aleksandr Solzhenitsyn	One Day in the Life of Ivan Denisovich
Sophocles	Oedipus the King
John Steinbeck	The Grapes of Wrath
Robert Louis Stevenson	Kidnapped
Bram Stoker	Dracula
Harriet Beecher Stowe	Uncle Tom's Cabin
Jonathan Swift	Gulliver's Travels
Henry David Thoreau	Walden
J.R.R. Tolkein	The Hobbit
Mark Twain	The Adventures of Huckleberry Finn
Jules Verne	Journey to the Center of the Earth
Kurt Vonnegut	Cat's Cradle
H.G. Wells	The Time Machine
Edith Wharton	The Age of Innocence
Walt Whitman	Leaves of Grass
Tennessee Williams	The Glass Menagerie
Richard Wright	Native Son

Your Courses Before College

The choices you make about your middle school and high school courses can influence where you will be accepted to college. As you enter high school, you will learn about what you need to study in order to receive a high school diploma. However, what you need to graduate from high school can be less than what you need to enter some of the more competitive colleges.

For example, you may need to take three years of general high school science in order to graduate. But many colleges may specifically require that you study biology and chemistry in high school.

Some students are taught at home rather than in a public or private school. If this is true for you, learn how your schooling may affect your college admission. Contact colleges that interest you for more information. The home schooling coordinator for your school district can also help.

In Chapter 9, we looked at different *levels* of courses, such as honors. Many high schools also offer different *programs*. For example, a college program is for students who intend to go on to college and a vocational track is for students who are heading to careers in areas such as plumbing, medical assistance, and auto repair. Some schools have tech-prep tracks for students entering high technology fields such as computer technology and science technology. Your school may also have a business track for office skills such as word processing. General education tracks do not provide specific college or career preparation.

If you are not in a college track, you can still go to college, but your choice of where to go may be limited. Understand your options before signing up for your ninth grade classes. Talk to a school counselor about the best plan of action for you. For example, you may be able to combine college track courses with vocational studies.

What other choices will I have in high school?
Not all of your high school courses are required. Just as in college, you can choose some electives. Colleges will be interested to see which electives you choose. Some are every bit as challenging as your required classes. Others challenge you less, but let you develop long-term skills (computer keyboarding) or express yourself creatively (choir and art). Try to get a sense of what mix of courses are of most interest to the colleges where you might be applying.

Do not overlook computers and foreign languages. Colleges do not expect all incoming students to be computer scientists. But they do prefer students who are computer literate—students who can use computers with some ease.

You may have the chance to be a foreign exchange student in high school. You would travel to another country and live with a family for anywhere from several weeks to an entire school year. This experience can be a wonderful opportunity to practice your foreign language skills and experience another culture.

As our world becomes increasingly small, the ability to communicate in another language grows in importance. Many colleges prefer students who study a foreign language in middle and high school. In fact, many require you to show a certain level of skill in a foreign language. You should strongly consider getting a head start well before you graduate from high school.

Should I graduate early from high school? At some high schools, you can graduate in three years rather than four by completing more courses each year. This option shows your commitment to your studies and lets you get a jump start on college. However, you may sacrifice many of the extra-curricular activities that high school offers and that help you round out your background. (You also lose a year of saving for college.) Before you choose this option, carefully weigh both sides.

What are gifted and talented programs? Many school districts have special programs for their best students. These programs start as early as elementary school. They often give students the chance to work at a higher level and, in many cases, to keep moving ahead at their own pace. If you find that certain subjects (or all of your courses) come very easily to you and that you are receiving the highest grades with little effort, you may want to talk to your parents, teachers, and school counselor about whether you should be evaluated for gifted and talented courses.

You can find books describing summer learning opportunities for students your age in the college guide section of many bookstores.

Do colleges offer special programs for kids? Many do. Lots of colleges have special programs for juniors and seniors. And many colleges now offer programs for freshmen and sophomores, as well as for elementary and middle school students. To find out more, contact the admissions offices at nearby colleges. In particular, look at programs that nearby community colleges offer. They have a strong commitment to serving their local community, particularly during the summer.

Michigan's Lansing Community College (LCC) has several programs for younger students. Summer sports camps are available for kids as young as first grade. High school juniors and seniors can participate in the dual enrollment program, taking college credit courses at LCC while finishing high school requirements. Freshmen and sophomores can apply for the special admissions program, which allows them to take college courses. The Saturday School program reaches gifted and talented students in both elementary and middle schools, providing seven-week courses in arts, science, math, and geography.

ADDITIONAL ACTIVITIES

How do you spend your time when you are not in class? If you are someone who comes home and just watches hours of television without much thought, now is the time to change your habits.

Girl Scouts of the U.S.A. have a strong interest in career opportunity awareness. They sponsor many activities from athletics to zoology.

You can choose all sorts of ways to spend these hours productively: playing sports, performing, creating art, or joining clubs. Many activities available through school are also available in your community: playing soccer in a neighborhood league, acting in a play sponsored by your church or temple, or becoming active with groups like Boy Scouts of America.

Another way to be active is through volunteer work. When you are old enough you can help out at the local hospital. You can help publicize a rally for a local political candidate. You can help serve meals at a local shelter.

In addition you can get a job—or create one for yourself. Babysitting, delivering papers, shoveling snow, and, when you are older, working at a restaurant, department store, or office all provide valuable experience as well as money that can be put toward college.

Any and all of these activities will improve your chances for getting into the college you want. You develop interests and skills that carry over into other parts of your life. But the real reason for participating in these activities is not to help you get into college. The most important reason for you to participate in these activities is simply that they enrich your life.

PREPARING FOR COLLEGE COSTS

One of the things that you can do at any time is start saving for college. Even if you get a lot of financial aid when you get to college, you will still need money to pay for day-to-day expenses or for major purchases such as a computer. As we noted earlier, if you decide not to go to college, you will still have saved money that can help you in other ways.

Suppose you are ten years old and start saving $5 per week in a savings account. You could have over $2,500 by the time you turn eighteen. While that may not pay your tuition, it will help a lot with books and supplies.

One of the other things you can do early on is to start looking into the types of scholarships and grants that are available. When you are actually in the process of applying to colleges, your life can be hectic. You may not really have time then to look into scholarships. Spending time now will give you a better chance of finding some of the more unusual grants that often go unused each year because no one applies for them.

You can also make contacts with some local organizations that award money to students from the area. Suppose a service club gives out a grant each year. If you have worked with them over several years as a volunteer, the club's members will know who you are. You may then have an advantage for winning the grant.

In short: The sooner you start to plan for college costs, the more prepared you will be.

DEVELOPING A PLAN

Between now and the time you go to college, you will be working with a lot of information. You will be gathering information about colleges and career opportunities, sources of financial aid, and the different college entrance exams. You'll be building a record, not only of grades, but also of books you've read, your activities, places you've visited, volunteer work, and paid work. You will be thinking about and evaluating your goals and your preferences. And you will also want to set financial goals to help pay for college.

You can choose all sorts of ways to stay on top of this information. What is important is that you develop an overall plan. Having a plan doesn't mean having a strict program or schedule that you must follow at all times. It does mean that you are an active participant in your own future. Choices that you make have consequences, for better or for worse.

*Rutgers University in New Jersey has a four-year guide—*My Academic Progress—*that helps you and your parents track specific goals and achievements during your high school years. Many other colleges also have planning guides and checklists that are available to students.*

Few people achieve their goals by luck alone. Some people may seem lucky, but in almost all cases, their success is built on self-discipline and a lot of effort.

Making a chart may be the best way to develop your plan. Create a checklist of what you want to accomplish each year—colleges to visit, how much to save, classes to take, habits to develop, skills to acquire, activities in which to participate, information to gather, tests to take, and so forth. Good choices help you keep doors open. Having a plan tailored to your needs and goals is the best way to stay in charge of your future!

☞ THE ROAD AHEAD

We began this book by telling you that college is a bridge to the future—your future! We hope we've been successful in answering many of your basic questions about college and helping you identify where you can go to learn more about the opportunities ahead of you.

The road ahead of you is an exciting one! As you travel it, we want to end our portion of your trip with three overall thoughts.

1. If you truly want to go to college, you *can* go and you *will* go. Do not let anyone tell you that you cannot go to college, no matter what reason they give you.

2. Do not let your financial resources stop you from thinking about college or applying. *First get accepted*; then find a way to pay for it.

3. The journey is as important as the destination. *How you get there*—what you learn, the skills you develop, the experiences you encounter, and the friends you make—*matters*. We wish you well.

4-1-4 — college calendar made up of a four-month term followed by one month of separate study and another four-month term

4-4-1 — college calendar made up of two four-month terms followed by one month of separate study

accreditation — proof that a college and its programs meet educational standards established by government or professional organizations

ACT — American College Testing; college entrance exam that tests students' skills in English, mathematics, reading, and science reading

administration — the group of people who run a college; group often includes the president, vice presidents, deans, and directors

admissions office — the college office that provides information and assistance to students interested in applying to the college; also the office that determines who will be accepted

Advanced Placement course — special high school courses taught at a college level; see also *AP Exam*

Advanced Placement Exam — see *AP Exam*

advisor — teacher or counselor who is assigned to help students choose their major and select their courses; students meet with their advisors at least once each term to prepare for the next term

affiliation — the relationship a college has with a particular group or organization, for example, with a religious denomination

alumni — the graduates of a college or any other educational institution; an individual graduate is called an *alumnus* or *alumna*

AP Exam — standardized test given nationally to students who have completed special high school classes taught at the college level

application fee — the fee most colleges charge to process your application form

assessment — a test or evaluation

associate's degree — degree given for completion of two-year program

bachelor's degree — degree given for completion of four-year program

board of trustees — the group with overall responsibility for a college; also called *board of directors*

branch campus — an additional campus of a college, other than the main campus

campus — a college's physical surroundings; its buildings and grounds

career center — location on campus where students can get a wide variety of information, advice, and assistance about employment

career counselor — someone who provides advice to students about job opportunities and how their interests and skills fit different careers

catalog — a book that describes a college's requirements, rules, and courses in detail

certificate — recognition that student has completed specific training or study in a specialized area

class rank — a measure of a student's academic performance compared to all other students in the same grade at the same school

college — school after high school, usually four-year programs leading to bachelor's degrees; see also *community college* and *university*

college calendar — the way in which a college divides its school year into terms; most often semesters, trimesters, and quarters

college entrance exams — standardized tests used to measure skills important for college success; many colleges require applicants to take at least one; most common are the SAT and the ACT

college fair — a special event where you get informational materials and speak with representatives from many different colleges

Common Application — an application form accepted by many private colleges; saves students time when they apply

community college — school after high school that offers programs leading to associate's degrees and certificates; full-time programs can usually be completed in two years; sometimes called *junior college*

consortium — a group of colleges that allow students at one college to take advantage of courses and facilities at the other colleges

cooperative education — a program combining studies with practical work experience, sometimes paid, in a student's chosen field; also called *co-op program*

commuter — a student who travels to and from college each day

competitive admission — applicants must meet or exceed specific standards; qualified applicants are then compared to determine who will be admitted

core courses — see *general education courses*

credit — a measure of how much a particular course counts toward completing overall graduation requirements; usually based on the number of hours a course meets each week; often used to calculate tuition; also called *credit hour*

dean — a person responsible for a major portion of the college

degree — the title a college grants to students who complete specific programs of study; most common are bachelor's degree (four-year college) and associate's degree (two-year college); advanced studies can lead to master's degrees and doctor's degrees

department — a group of professors who teach in the same subject area; the head of the department is often called the *department chair*

developmental studies — programs that help develop a student's basic skills, bringing them up to a college level; also called *remedial studies*

discipline — a subject area such as English, biology, or psychology

discussion group — a group of students who meet regularly (usually weekly) to discuss topics from the course; usually headed by a faculty member or graduate assistant

distribution requirements — courses that students are required to take from a variety of different subject areas before they can graduate

diversity — differences in personal characteristics, background, and experience, including race, religion, gender, and geography

division — a group of related departments that often make up a unit within the college, e.g., the natural sciences division

doctorate — an advanced degree; also called *doctor's degree*

dormitory — a building that houses students who live on a college campus; also called *residence hall*

electives — courses student elect to take, but are not required to take; can be general (students choose any course they want) or specific (students choose from a selected group of courses)

e-mail — electronic mail, which people send through their computers

entrance exam — see *college entrance exam*

entry services — office that assists students thinking about attending a particular college as well as students who are just beginning college

ESL — English as a Second Language; refers to special services and classes for students whose native language is not English

estimated family contribution (EFC) — the amount that, according to a government formula, your family should be able to pay toward your college costs

ethnicity — ethnic background; the common national, religious, racial, tribal, language, or cultural backgrounds that bond groups of people

exchange program — a program that allows students at one college to attend a different college for one or more terms

extracurricular activities — activites in which a student participates outside of class

faculty — the teachers at a college, e.g., professors, associate and assistant professors, lecturers, and instructors

FAFSA — Free Application for Federal Student Aid; the form students use to apply for financial assistance from the government

fees — charges for particular services, equipment, or facilities

field studies — studies that take place outside traditional classrooms and labs, in a setting where subjects can be studied firsthand

financial aid — money provided to a student to help pay for college

financial aid package — the combination of grants, scholarships, loans, and work-study that a student receives to help pay for college

first-generation student — a college student whose parents did not attend college

fraternity — national membership organization for men, with individual chapters at various colleges

freshman — a student who is in the first year of college

gender — male or female

general education courses — courses that are required of all students in order to graduate, regardless of the students' primary field of study

grade point average (GPA) — a summary of all of a student's grades for a term, a year, or several years

graduate student — a student who has already earned a bachelor's degree and is continuing to study at an advanced level

graduate assistant — a graduate student who helps a faculty member by teaching, grading, leading discussions, or conducting research

grant — a financial award that does not need to be repaid

home page — a visual location or address on the Internet

independent study — an opportunity to study a topic in depth outside of a traditional classroom, usually working individually with a teacher

infirmary — the health facility on campus

interdisciplinary — courses or major combining more than one subject

internship — program that lets students apply studies in a work setting

intramural sports — athletic programs that enable students within a college to compete against each other; open to all students

job placement — the office that brings together employers and students

junior — a student who is in the third year of a four-year college

lab — setting where students conduct experiments; also settings where students can practice specific skills, e.g., a computer lab

learning resource center — see *library*

lecture — a class setting where teacher speaks in front of students

loan — financial assistance that must be repaid

main campus — usually the largest campus of a college where the greatest number of resources and services are located

major — the area of study in which a student chooses to specialize

master's degree — an advanced degree following a bachelor's degree

merit-based aid — financial assistance based on a student's talents

minor — a second area of study that a student emphasizes

multimedia — combining two or more types of media such as film, videotapes, audiotapes, computer, and CD-ROM

National Candidates' Reply Date — May 1, a common deadline by which students must notify colleges where they will attend

NCAA — National Collegiate Athletic Association; organization that oversees college athletic programs

need-based aid — financial assistance based on a student's ability to pay for college

open admissions — applicants are admitted with few requirements

orientation — program designed to introduce students to the college

placement test — exams given after students are admitted; helps to determine which courses students need to take

private college — an independent college set up by individuals or organizations; receives little taxpayer support

PROFILE — a form many private colleges require students to complete in order to qualify for need-based aid

proprietary — a privately-controlled school; specializes in areas such as business, technical, and vocational training

PSAT/NMSQT — Preliminary Scholastic Achievement Test/National Merit Scholarship Qualifying Test; provides practice for the SAT and enables students to qualify for scholarship programs

public college — a college set up with government support; receives strong taxpaper support

quarter — a college term lasting about 11 weeks; full-time students usually attend three quarter terms each year

recruitment — the process of finding students to apply to the college

registrar — the person responsible for registration and for maintaining student records

registration — the process of signing up or enrolling in classes

resident assistant — someone who supervises a portion of a dormitory

residence hall — see *dormitory*

room and board — the cost of housing (room) and meals (board)

ROTC — Reserve Officer Training Corps; a program that combines military training with college studies

SAT I — Scholastic Achievement Test; college entrance exam that tests students' verbal and math skills

SAT II — formerly the Achievement Tests; college entrance exam that test students' skills in specific subject areas

schedule of classes — a listing of courses offered each term along with dates, times, and locations; also called *class schedule*

scholarship — a financial award that does not need to be repaid

selective admissions — applicants must either meet or exceed specific standards to qualify for admission

selectivity —the level of difficulty involved in getting into a specific college; levels include open, selective, and competitive admissions

self-paced classes — classes that let students work at their own speed

semester — a college term lasting about 16 to 18 weeks; full-time students attend two semesters each year

seminar — a small discussion-oriented class, usually for upperclassmen

senior — a student in the final year of a four-year college

sophomore — a student in the second year of college

sorority — national membership organization for women, with individual chapters at various colleges

student union — the building that is central to student activities and services; often includes dining hall, mailroom, and bookstore

student-faculty ratio — the number of students for every teacher

syllabus — a course outline provided by the teacher

teaching assistant — see *graduate assistant*

term — a period of time during which courses are taught

transcript — a summary of a student's academic record

transfer — the process of switching from one college to another

trimester — a college term lasting about 15 weeks; full-time students attend two out of three trimesters each year

tuition — the portion of college costs that pays directly for classes

two-year college — see *community college*

undergraduate — a student who has not yet completed graduation requirements nor earned a bachelor's (or associate's) degree

university — institution of higher learning that usually combines one or more colleges with other schools, e.g., medical or law school

upperclassmen — juniors and seniors at a college

viewbook — a booklet that provides both photographs and general information about a college

waiver — permission not to pay an expense or to repay a loan

work-study — financial assistance program that provides students with jobs, usually on campus

MAP OF THE UNITED STATES

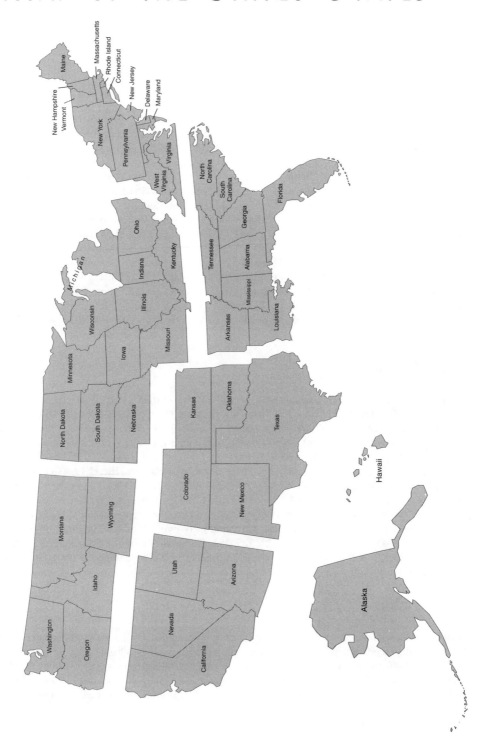

CREDITS

PHOTO CREDITS

CHAPTER 1— p. 5 courtesy of the University of Nebraska—Lincoln **p. 8** courtesy of Flathead Valley Community College **p. 10 (top)** photo Dean Color, courtesy of Adirondack Community College **p. 10** (bottom) photo Angel Art, courtesy of University at Buffalo Publications Department **p. 16** photo Colby Communications **CHAPTER 2 — p. 20** photo Mark Swisher **p. 21** photo Mark Swisher **p. 25** courtesy of Paul Bither **p. 27** photo Mark Swisher **p. 30** photo Carol Rosegg, courtesy of Gregory Jbara **p. 31** © 1989 by Don Putnam, courtesy of Almo Music Corp. **p. 33** photo Mark Swisher **p. 34** photo Mark Swisher **CHAPTER 3 — p. 35** photo Mark Swisher **p. 52** photo Mark Swisher **CHAPTER 4 — p. 53** photo Colby Communications **p. 54** courtesy of Miami-Dade Community College **p. 55** photo Franklin Muñoz, courtesy of UTEP News and Publications **CHAPTER 5 — p. 65** photo Mark Swisher **CHAPTER 6 — p. 87** photo Colby Communications **p. 90** photo Mark Swisher **p. 93** photo Colby Communications **p. 94** photo Mark Swisher **p. 97** courtesy of Dale Murphy **p. 99** photo Colby Communications **p. 100** photo Colby Communications **p. 101** photo Colby Communications **CHAPTER 7 — p. 105** photo Colby Communications **p. 117** photo Mark Swisher **CHAPTER 8 — p. 123** photo Colby Communications **p. 125** photo courtesy of CBS Sports **CHAPTER 12 — p. 193** photo Colby Communications **p. 196** courtesy of Howard Community College **p. 208** photo Mark Swisher **CHAPTER 14 — p. 234** courtesy of Gina Dounelis

ILLUSTRATION CREDITS

AST Research, Inc. © 1994: pages 1, 14 (upper left), 14 (upper right), 14 (bottom left), 59, 76 (bottom), 79 (bottom), 81a, 81b, 85 (top), 248, 259. **Corel Corporation** © 1994: pages 4, 5, 6, 7, 13, 19 (upper left), 19 (bottom right), 24, 29, 32, 37, 44, 56, 58, 60, 61, 72, 75 (top), 77a, 77b, 77c, 80 (top), 81c, 82 (bottom), 84 (top), 84 (middle), 85 (bottom), 86, 95, 96, 99, 107 (bottom), 111, 115 (top), 116 (bottom), 118, 121, 130, 131, 132, 136, 139, 143, 149, 154, 157, 160, 162, 163, 180, 184, 188, 190, 195, 201, 209, 213, 216, 220, 224, 227, 230, 232, 233, 243, 244, 245, 259. **Image Club Graphics, Inc.** © 1994: pages 14 (center), 19 (upper right), 19 (center), 22, 40, 42, 43, 47, 62, 78 (middle), 79 (middle), 85 (middle), 100, 103, 107, 115 (bottom), 116 (top), 122, 129, 141, 146, 158, 161, 172, 175, 176, 178, 187, 215, 217, 228, 229, 231, 235, 238, 246. **Microsoft Works, Inc.** © 1993: pages 14 (bottom right), 74 (top). **One Mile Up, Inc.** © 1994: pages 28, 46, 50, 51, 74 (bottom), 75 (bottom), 76 (top), 78 (top), 80 (bottom), 81 (bottom), 88, 102, 126, 137, 145, 168, 185, 189, 199, 221, 225, 259. **Techpool Studios** © 1994: page 19 (bottom left). **Totem Graphics, Inc.** © 1994: pages 3, 41, 67, 75 (middle), 77d, 78 (bottom), 79 (top), 80 (middle), 82 (top), 84 (bottom), 204.

ADDITIONAL CREDITS

Many of the charts and tables are based on information compiled from a variety of sources, including college catalogs, college home pages, and interviews with representatives from college admissions offices, financial aid offices, and public relations offices. In addition, information was provided by the U.S. Department of Labor and the U.S. Department of Education, especially the National Library of Education. Adam Joshua Smargon (recycler@ufl.edu) provided much of the information used on pages 224-225.

INDEX

ABOUT THE AUTHORS

BARBARA C. GREENFELD has been Director of Admissions at Howard Community College in Columbia, Maryland, for the past ten years. She is an honors graduate of the University of Maryland and received her M.S. with Honors from Johns Hopkins University. She has received both local and national awards for her achievements. She has developed numerous special programs at the college; these include the innovative James W. Rouse Scholars Program, the Summer Honors Program for High School Students, and the Annual High Tech Learning Expo. Throughout her career, she has worked extensively with students of all ages—at both the college and grade school level—and has special expertise working with students who have learning disabilities. She is a contributing author of *Student Handbook: Volume 4*, published by The Southwestern Company.

ROBERT A. WEINSTEIN has spent over a decade in educational publishing. He is an honors graduate of Colby College and received his M.B.A. from Harvard University. As an editor for McGraw-Hill College Division and other publishers, he has visited hundreds of colleges across the country and has published dozens of successful texts as well as numerous supplements using a wide range of media. He has edited many books in the HarperCollins College Outline Series and is the author of a variety of materials aimed at helping high school students make a successful transition to college.

LET'S HEAR FROM YOU!

THE AUTHORS OF **THE KIDS' COLLEGE ALMANAC** WOULD LOVE TO HEAR FROM YOU WITH ANY QUESTIONS AND SUGGESTIONS THAT YOU WOULD LIKE TO SEE ADDRESSED IN FUTURE EDITIONS.

YOU CAN WRITE TO THE AUTHORS IN CARE OF

GERSON PUBLISHING COMPANY
P.O. BOX 525
MATAWAN, NJ 07747

IN ADDITION, KEEP YOUR EYES OPEN FOR A SUPPLEMENTARY BOOK, **THE KIDS' COLLEGE ALMANAC ACTIVITY BOOK,** AVAILABLE STARTING IN FALL 1996. FOR MORE INFORMATION, WRITE TO GERSON PUBLISHING COMPANY.

ORDERING MORE COPIES

IF YOU WANT MORE COPIES OF **THE KIDS' COLLEGE ALMANAC**, CHECK WITH YOUR LOCAL BOOKSTORE OR ORDER DIRECTLY FROM US. YOU CAN ORDER FROM GERSON PUBLISHING COMPANY BY SENDING YOUR CHECK OR MONEY ORDER TO THE ADDRESS BELOW. (DO NOT SEND CASH.) PLEASE PRINT YOUR NAME AND ADDRESS.

EACH COPY IS $16.95. INCLUDE $3.00 SHIPPING AND HANDLING FOR ONE BOOK, AND $1.00 FOR EACH ADDITIONAL BOOK. NEW JERSEY RESIDENTS MUST ADD 6% SALES TAX. DISCOUNT RATES ARE AVAILABLE FOR BULK ORDERS (TEN OR MORE COPIES) -- CONTACT THE PUBLISHER FOR MORE INFORMATION. THANK YOU!!

GERSON PUBLISHING COMPANY
P.O. BOX 525
MATAWAN, NJ 07747